NO FEAR GRAMMAR

Titles in the **NO FEAR** Skills Series

No Fear Algebra

No Fear Grammar

No Fear Spanish

No Fear Vocabulary

NO FEAR GRAMMAR

A BARNES & NOBLE PUBLICATION

This edition published by Spark Publishing

Spark Publishing
A Division of SparkNotes LLC
120 Fifth Avenue, 8th Floor
New York, NY 10011

ISBN 1-4114-0135-2

Please submit changes or report errors to *www.sparknotes.com/errors*

Written by Liesa Abrams

Printed and bound in Canada

A Barnes & Noble Publication

CONTENTS

INTRODUCTION
MEET ME, ARIANNA MARTINEZ

HEY THERE!

My name is Arianna Martinez, and I'm a grammar geek. Yes, it's true. My best friend, Rosita, wasn't the only one to tease me about my knack for grammar, but she was the first to take it all back the second she realized just how important my skills were—like, getting-the-guy-of-her-dreams important. Now you're listening, right? Well, you're going to have to keep reading if you want the full scoop.

Let me just say this for now: Getting a handle on grammar can be a huge help for a lot of different reasons. Maybe it's not always the one missing link between you and the love of your life (hold on, hold on—I told you I'd get to that part soon!), but even on a regular day, good grammar can make a difference in your life.

OH YEAH?

Take school, for starters, since that's where you—unfortunately, I know—spend a whole lot of your time. Knowing how to say and write things the right way is a big step in getting the teacher on your side. You'll be able to express yourself much better in any class, not just English, and you'll wow your teachers with your top-notch sentences.

Okay, you're saying, so the teachers will love me, but what about the people who, like, actually matter? Well, even when my friends used to tease me, they would always admit that deep down they were a little jealous of all the stuff I knew. Good grammar is a great party trick to help you sound super-smart about any topic, because when you're speaking or writing correctly, you sound mighty impressive.

Plus, there are always the college entrance exams (insert groan here): the SAT or ACT. Like it or not, how you do on these tests plays a big role in whether you'll get into your favorite college, and I for one don't want my score to hold me back from my dream school.

HELP!

Now that you're starting to see how much grammar matters, you might be a little freaked, the way Rosita was when she showed up at my house one Saturday afternoon a few months ago (I'm getting to that, trust me). Rosita's a smart girl, but she was pretty confused about grammar, probably because a lot of people make it sound way more complicated than it has to be. I sat her down and gave her some basic lessons on the most important rules, tips, and tricks for being a grammar pro, and I figured it might help you to check out those lessons, too.

If you want, you can read this book from cover to cover, which is how I like to read things. Or you can skip around and just jump to whatever parts of grammar you most need to know at the moment. Each chapter gives you a topic, and there are lots of different sections inside each chapter on rules and lessons within that topic.

So keep reading to hear my story and, I hope, learn something along the way.

NO FEAR GRAMMAR

1

CHAPTER 1
CLAUSES AND PHRASES

It was a Saturday afternoon in October, and there I was at home, minding my own business and reading *The Crucible* for English class, when my best friend, Rosita, showed up at my front door looking totally frantic.

"You have to help me," Rosita begged. "I'm in major trouble!"

A quick glance behind Rosita assured me that there were no knife-wielding maniacs chasing her, and my ears detected no wailing sirens signaling that police officers were on the way to make an arrest. I assumed this emergency was a typical Rosita version of a crisis.

In other words, a cute guy was very likely involved.

"Come on in," I told her with a sigh, realizing I wasn't going to see the end of Act I in *The Crucible* anytime soon.

Moments later, Rosita was flopped across my bed, her long, straight, dark hair spread out around her on my pillow. "Arianna, he was *so* cute," she moaned. On our way upstairs she'd confirmed my suspicion: She'd met a guy at our high school's football game. He was a junior at River Dell High, which had creamed our school, Paramus, and he played in their marching band. She'd met him through our friend Rich, who plays the drums for the Paramus band.

"This guy is it, Arianna, I swear," Rosita said. "I know I say that a lot, but Charlie's different. Tall, gorgeous, pale skin. Really pale skin, actually. We just talked for a few minutes, but I've never felt like this about anyone."

"Charlie? His name's Charlie?" I asked. My heart jumped a beat. Charlie, from River Dell High. . . .

Rosita sat up, giving me a funny look. "Yeah, it's Charlie," she said. "So?"

"Nothing," I said quickly. It couldn't be him. There had to be other Charlies who lived in that area, right? "So what's the problem, anyway?" I asked. "If you guys had this magical moment together, what are you doing here? I'm surprised you're not already getting ready for your first date."

I guess I should explain why I would say something like that. See, Rosita has this–I don't know what you'd call it–talent, maybe? The second she spots a guy she likes, he's all hers. (And, yeah, I know, if there were a book out there on how to get someone you like to fall for you right away, you'd be reading that one instead of this one, but unfortunately there's no such thing.) For the rest of us mere mortals, crushes can be a killer, but Rosita usually doesn't face much of a challenge.

"Here's where you come in," Rosita admitted. She got up and came over to the edge of the bed, right next to where I was sitting at my desk chair. "See, Charlie had to go when their band director called him back over, and we didn't exchange numbers or anything. So I asked Rich, and he said he'd give me Charlie's email address. But he warned me that Charlie's one of those English types, like you, and it drives him crazy when people don't use good grammar in emails."

"I know. It's so annoying!" I blurted out. "I mean, how hard is it to hit the shift key a couple of times and put in some capital letters at the beginning of your sentences? Or, God, even *write* some actual sentences?"

Rosita rolled her eyes. "I knew I came to the right person," she said. "Listen, I have this email I want to send Charlie, but I need you to help me write it so that it looks all right, okay? Please?"

"One condition," I warned.

"Anything," she said solemnly.

"No more eye-rolls," I said. "If we do this, then we do it right."

"Got it," she said. "Now work your magic, oh, queen of all things grammar."

I raised my eyebrows.

"What? Okay, okay, I'll be serious," she said. "I promise."

Wow. It looked like Rosita really did like this Charlie guy.

THE SENTENCE

The first thing I did was have Rosita type up a draft of the email on the computer. It was a good thing she'd asked for my help, especially if Charlie really was a grammar snob. Her sentences–if you could call them that–were a mess. It wasn't clear whom her sentences were about, or what was happening in them. A sentence needs two things to do its job.

First, it needs a subject–*something* or *someone* to talk about. (Don't we all!) Like a good gossip, a sentence should name names, usually in the form of a **noun**, which is a person, place, thing, or idea. Like this:

Rosita.

A good gossip also reports on what the person, place, thing, or idea *did* (usually in the form of a **verb**):

Met an incredible guy.

Combine the two parts . . . and we have our juicy sentence:

Rosita met an incredible guy.

So now you know a sentence needs a subject and a verb. In grammar-speak, Rosita is the **subject** of the sentence. The verb *met*, and everything that comes after it, is the **predicate**.

COMPOUND SUBJECTS AND PREDICATES

Here's a bit of trickiness: Sometimes a sentence wants to gossip about more than one person, place, or thing. In other words, sometimes a sentence needs more than one subject. That's okay with me, or with any other friendly neighborhood grammar guru. Look at this example:

Rosita and I like good grammar for different reasons.

Both *Rosita* and *I* are the main actors in that sentence. Like the best friends we are, we're sharing the verb *like*. When you put two subjects into a sentence, you've created a **compound subject**.

Sometimes, a subject does more than one thing. Look at this:

Rosita met and liked an incredible guy.

Here, Rosita did two things: She both met and liked a guy . . . who happened to be Charlie. Life, as well as this sentence, would be so much easier if she'd met him and left it at that! When you use two verbs, you create a **compound predicate**.

Whenever you have two subjects or two verbs, you should join them together with *and* or *or*. These little words are called **conjunctions**.

A SENTENCE BY ANY OTHER NAME . . .

Did you ever come up with a different name for yourself, just for fun? Our friend the sentence is also called an **independent clause.** This alias tells us something important: A sentence can stand alone, on its own, and shout out its meaning loud and clear, with no confusion.

SENTENCE FRAGMENTS

Now you know that a sentence needs a subject and a verb, and you can gossip as much as your little heart desires. People will look to you for information, because they know you've got all the facts.

Sometimes, sentences are incomplete. What could be worse than hearing enough of a piece of gossip to know that it's good but not enough to figure out who it's about? Here's an example:

Met an incredible guy.

It's just not fair, is it? Or check this out:

Rosita at the football game.

Agony! Both of these examples are missing something: One doesn't tell us *who,* and one doesn't tell us *what happened.* These examples tell us about a highly interesting action, or they name names, but not both. We call these teasers **sentence fragments.** Always make sure your sentences have both a subject and a verb.

SUBORDINATE CLAUSES

There's an even worse situation, when names get named and what the actors did gets reported, but you *still* don't know the whole story. Check this out:

Although Rosita met an incredible guy at the football game.

Okay, we know there's a hitch with Mr. Incredible because of that word *although.* Something's up, but we don't know what it is. We've got everything we need for a complete sentence, including a subject and a verb, but we don't have a complete thought. The tiny word *although* has robbed the sentence of its independence—all by itself, the sentence doesn't tell us what we need to know. We need more!

To make this fake sentence a real sentence, we need to add another subject and verb to explain what's up:

> Although Rosita met an incredible guy at the football game, she's worried she'll lose him if she doesn't improve her grammar.

Now the sentence tells us everything we need to know.

The sentence has independence. It delivers the whole thought. Remember: In grammar-speak, a stand-alone subject with a predicate is called an **independent clause**. It's totally unfair, but just because you have a clause doesn't mean you have a whole sentence. When you see a subject and a verb together but not a whole sentence, what you have is a **dependent** or **subordinate clause**. It relies on something else to get its meaning across.

Feeling a little woozy? Don't worry. We'll come back to subordinate clauses later. For now, just remember that even tiny words like *although, if,* or *until* can take away a clause's freedom to be a sentence.

END PUNCTUATION

It was right around here that Rosita tuned out. "I can't wait anymore," she said. "Let's send the email already! He probably forgot who I am by now!" I gave in, realizing that we would be there for a while if I finished my lesson on the sentence that day. So I told her we'd learn just one more important thing about a sentence: how to end it.

EASY ENDING

The easiest and most common way to end a sentence is with a period. Most sentences do—and *should*—end with periods. Here's a simple one:

> Sometimes I think I'll never meet someone.

GOT A QUESTION?

There are a couple of types of sentences that don't end with periods. Some of them end with question marks. Which ones? Yeah, I figured you already knew. *Questions* end with question marks. **Don't you wish all of grammar were this**

easy? (That was your example, by the way. I'm sneaky like that.)

CONTAIN YOURSELF!

I know, I know, all this talk of grammar has you bubbling over with excitement. You can barely hold it all in, which makes you want to *exclaim* with intense emotion. If you're looking for a way to help you do it, I have just the thing—the exclamation point.

Exclamation points end statements that express very strong feelings or urgent warnings, like:

I'll never meet someone!
Watch out!

Putting an exclamation point at the end of a sentence is almost like making that sentence scream to the reader, so if you want to play it cool, don't use them too often.

That's enough listening to me talk—it's time for you to take your new grammar know-how for a little test drive. See if you can fix up these sentences the same way I rescued Rosita's email.

Underline the main noun or nouns in the subject once and the main verb or verbs in the predicate twice. Then draw a line between the subject as a whole and the predicate. If the sentence is a fragment, rewrite it so that it has a subject and predicate.

1. My friend finally figured out the real purpose of grammar.

2. Good grammar skills and football games help you to meet guys.

3. Rosita, who was never a huge grammar fan, was afraid to write Charlie an email.

4. Because Rich warned Rosita about using good grammar.

5. Being a good friend, I agreed to give Rosita a little crash course in clauses.

6. A friendship that also helps your grammar is pretty rare.

7. Giving advice works both ways, though, with Rosita and me.

8. On the subject of clothes, Rosita has opinions to spare and shares them freely.

9. Her long hair flipped over her shoulder, Rosita rummages through my closet, talking about my sweaters but actually looking for something cool to borrow.

10. Rosita is talented at meeting guys and seldom sits home on a Saturday night, but she is never, ever the slightest bit stuck on herself.

* * * * *

Before we hit SEND on Rosita's email to Charlie, I made a few more tweaks just to be sure he'd really be impressed. It was funny: Even though the email was technically from Rosita, I'd started to feel like it was from both of us. I was just as worried as Rosita was about whether Charlie would write back.

Rosita couldn't thank me enough for my help, and she even agreed to loan me her new Toasters CD.

"I never thought you'd be grateful to me for lecturing you about grammar," I teased her.

"I guess I never realized how much I had to learn," she said. "Arianna, you're so awesome at this stuff. In fact, speaking of awesome . . ."

Uh-oh.

"If Charlie does write back, I'll need to respond to that email. And who knows how many more emails I'll have to send him? Maybe it'd be a good idea if we started at square one, and you could tell me everything I ever needed to know about grammar. Please? With Ben & Jerry's Cherry Garcia ice cream on top?"

Sometimes unsung talents like being good at grammar can get you into a heap of trouble.

CHAPTER 2
THE NOUN

I couldn't believe the world was really so small. How could this be happening? It was Sunday night, Rosita was back at my place, hanging out in my room, and right there on my nice, big seventeen-inch computer monitor was a face I recognized all too well: jet black hair, gelled back to expose a sharp widow's peak; glowing red eyes. . . . It was clearly Charlie Houston, the guy with whom I'd been completely obsessed during my entire seventh-grade year, before his family moved to River Dell and he switched schools.

"Isn't he gorgeous?" Rosita asked me.

I gulped. "Um–yeah."

Charlie hadn't really mourned our separation as much as I had. That was probably because he barely knew I existed. It was a totally one-sided crush, but it had been so intense that I couldn't help feeling as though he'd actually been sort of *mine*. I felt like I was starring in a bad teen movie: *Arianna's life was going along just fine . . . until the handsome guy from her past came back in the form of her best friend's crush.* Definitely blockbuster material.

I'd never mentioned Charlie to Rosita. She'd started at Paramus in ninth grade, and we'd had that instant, best-friend connection. But I'd never felt the need to update her on every detail of life before her. What was the point of embarrassing myself by telling her all about some guy who'd never returned my feelings, a guy who'd never really had a chance to return them, actually, since I was always too shy to say a word to him?

"So now you get it, right?" Rosita continued, somehow oblivious to my meltdown. "You know why my email had to be perfect, and why it's killing me that he hasn't written back yet. It's been almost twenty-four hours!"

I smiled in spite of myself. "Rosi, it's the weekend. Maybe he hasn't even checked his email. I know you're used to guys jumping the second you snap, but I don't think you have to worry too much that it's been a day since you sent Charlie an email."

"Yeah, yeah, okay." Rosita sighed, lying back on my bed. "I'm just glad we found that picture of him online, so you can see what he looks like."

I didn't say anything. I'd been suspicious ever since she first told me about Charlie yesterday, but now I knew for sure that he was Charlie Houston—*my* Charlie. (Who, I might add, hadn't changed the slightest bit since middle school.) I couldn't tell her the truth, though. What right did I have to keep the two of them apart if they liked each other? I'd had chances—tons of them—to go for him back in middle school. It wasn't Rosita's fault that I was such a wimp when it came to guys.

"So, do you think he'll write back?" she asked.

"Yes, I think he'll write back. Listen, this is ridiculous. We can't just sit here all night checking your email every ten seconds. Why don't we start those grammar lessons you said you wanted? How about we start with nouns? Nouns are fun."

"Yeah, fine, we'll do nouns." She sat up and reached across the bed to grab her notebook and pen from her backpack. "But Arianna?"

"Uh-huh?"

"Don't let me hear you use the word *fun* in the same breath as *grammar* ever again, okay?"

PARTS OF SPEECH

Which came first: the chicken or the egg? And you thought grammar was tricky! Let me ask an easier question. Which came first: words or sentences? Words did, of course. You can't have a sentence without them.

You know already that there are different kinds of words that do different things in a sentence. There are eight different kinds of words:

- nouns
- pronouns
- verbs
- adjectives
- adverbs
- prepositions
- conjunctions
- interjections

These are called **parts of speech**, and every single word in a sentence falls into one of those categories.

When you look at a sentence, you can break it apart and give a label to every word . . . if, you know, you like doing stuff like that.

WHAT NOUNS ARE

Rosita	New Jersey
computer	love

The four items above have something in common: They're all things that make up my world. Look around—see any others? I see:

my pen	a map of Paramus
my shoe	my sister, Marie

And how about things you feel? I, for instance, feel *anxiety* about typing Rosita's next email. Our pile of words is like a crazy quilt now:

Rosita	New Jersey
computer	love
pen	shoe
map	Paramus
sister	Marie
anxiety	email

But still they have one thing in common: All of the people, places, things, and ideas that make up our world are called **nouns**.

COMMON VS. PROPER

Look at our list again. Some of the nouns start with capital letters, and some don't. I didn't capitalize willy-nilly. If I did, a sentence might look something like this:

I helped rosita write an Email on my Computer to charlie, despite my Jealousy.

Wrong, all wrong. Here's the deal:

- Use capital letters for names, places, and brand names: Arianna, America, Arby's.
- Use lowercase letters for everything else: friend, country, restaurant.

Nouns that need a capital letter are called **proper nouns**. They name specific and often unique people, places, or things. You should always capitalize nouns relating to religions, nationalities, languages, and organizations:

- I'm learning about *Buddhism*.
- The two *Americans* flew to Rome.
- I speak *English*.
- My dad is a member of the *Parent-Teacher Association*.

Nouns that aren't so specific and don't need capital letters are called **common nouns**. There's only one Rosita, but there are lots of *girls*; there's only one Paramus, but there are lots of *towns*.

CONCRETE VS. ABSTRACT

Take a look at these words:

Charlie	love
friend	jealousy
computer	flirtation
school	anxiety

What do they have in common? Obviously, they all play roles in the soap opera I like to call *My Life*. More important, they're all nouns—each one of them is a person, place, thing, or idea.

But nouns in the first list—*Charlie*, *friend*, *computer*, and *school*—are very different from the nouns in the second list—*love*, *jealousy*, *flirtation*, and *anxiety*. The nouns in the first group are things you can reach out and touch (unless one of them happens to be your best friend's crush!). You can't touch the things in the second group.

We call nouns you can touch **concrete nouns**. The ones you can't touch are called **abstract nouns**.

SINGLE VS. PLURAL

The hardest part about singular and plural nouns is learning how to turn a singular one into a plural one. For most nouns, you just add an *-s* or *-es* to get the job done. For example:

computer becomes *computer**s***
town becomes *town**s***
crush becomes *crush**es***

> ### -*S* VS. -*ES*
>
> You really have to use your ear to help you out on this one. Try the word out in your head with just an *-s* and see if it sounds okay. Some words won't sound right, and those words need *-es*. In general, nouns that end in *s, sh, ss, ch, x,* or *z* will need an *-es*. Also, some nouns that end in *o*, like *potato, tomato*, and *hero*, get the special *-es* treatment.

EXCEPTIONS

Some nouns are high-maintenance. They make you go to extra trouble to take them from singular to plural. It's hard to get all of them down at first, but eventually you'll learn to recognize the exceptions, I promise!

One exception: nouns that end in *us*, like *cactus* or *alumnus*. For these words, you take away the *-us* and slap on a little *-i* to make the plural nouns: *cacti* and *alumni*.

Another exception: nouns that end in *-f* or *-fe*. These nouns often lose the *-f* or *-fe* and gain a *-ves*, as in these examples:

*lea**f*** becomes *lea**ves***
*li**fe*** becomes *li**ves***

There are also some nouns that stay the same when they're made plural, like *deer*, *sheep*, and *bison*. Some nouns don't change from singular to plural because they name things that can't be counted, like *dust* or *peace*.

Then there are the wild-card nouns that seem to take on wacky plural forms

Then there are the wild-card nouns that seem to take on wacky plural forms just for the fun of it:

mouse	mice
tooth	teeth
foot	feet
louse	lice

Argh! There's usually some kind of logic behind these switches, though, and after some time you start to catch on. For instance, the two *o*s in *tooth* become two *e*s, the same way they do when you turn *foot* into *feet*. And the *ouse* in *mouse* becomes *ice*, the same way it does when you take a *louse* and turn it into *lice*.

Y ME?

Just when it's starting to seem as if there are no rules you can count on in the land of plural nouns, along comes the *y* rule. This one's clean and simple. If a singular noun ends in the letter *y*, just look to the second to last letter of the word. If it's a vowel, you simply add an *-s*.

toy becomes *toy***s**

If the second to last letter is a consonant, take the *-y* away and add *-ies*.

penny becomes *penn***ies**

Whew! Now that we're done with plural nouns, we can go on to some more *nounology* (warning—made-up word alert!).

NOUN CLAUSES

By now, you know what a noun is and does. Let's have some fun with one of my favorite nouns: *roller coaster*. Let's make *roller coaster* the subject of a sentence:

A roller coaster makes my stomach do crazy things.

Let's rewrite that sentence a different way:

What a roller coaster does to my stomach is alarming.

Roller coaster is still there, but it's not the subject anymore. You know that the verb is *is* . . . but what's the subject? The roller coaster itself isn't alarming. *What*

the sentence. That group of words is also a noun. Surprised? Don't be. A noun can be a single word OR a collection of words. If a noun is made up of more than one word, it's called a **noun clause**.

POSSESSIVE NOUNS

Rosita and I both own a lot of cool stuff, and we lend things to each other all the time. And my own stuff is constantly getting mixed up with Marie's. So how do we know whose stuff is whose? Sometimes we have to remind each other who possesses what. That CD on my desk is Rosita's CD. On my feet are Marie's socks. Later, I plan to borrow Marie's purse, too.

Notice anything about the way I described who owns the things around me? I added *'s* to the nouns *Marie* and *Rosita*. To show that they possess the CD, socks, and purse, I made them *possessive*.

Possessive nouns show ownership of some other noun. To make a noun possessive, add an apostrophe.

- Add an -*s* if it's singular.
- Don't add an -*s* if it's plural.

For example:

Rosita's crush
two best friends' crush

If a singular noun ends in *s*, such as the name *James*, add an apostrophe and an -*s*.

If it sounds awkward, however, you can leave off that extra -*s*:

James's book
Sophocles' ideas

Of course, the two best friends' crush thing is purely an example for the sake of grammar here. Because for two best friends to share "ownership" of one crush . . . well, that would just be very, very bad news.

END OF THE LINE

When you have a noun phrase, like *two best friends*, the apostrophe goes after the last word of the phrase.

ARTICLES: A, AN, AND THE

Since I'm an excellent friend, let me give you a suggestion: Don't get yourself into a situation like the one I'm in now.

Just for fun, let me give you that suggestion again. But I'm going to leave out something important:

Since I'm excellent friend, let me give you suggestion: Don't get yourself into situation like one I'm in now.

Notice something strange? Sure you do. I forgot those important little words that come before nouns in a sentence: *a*, *an*, and *the*. You use these words all the time.

When you don't know any specifics about a noun, you use *a* or *an*, as long as the noun is singular and can be counted. For example:

RIGHT: *a* computer
RIGHT: *an* annoyance
WRONG: *an* advice *(you can't count **advice**)*
WRONG: *a* problems *(**problems** is plural)*

WHAT THEY'RE CALLED

The is called a **definite article.** *A* and *an* are called **indefinite articles.** You'll see the indefinite article *a* much more often than its good friend *an* because you use *a* before a noun that begins with a consonant, which includes most nouns. But whenever a noun begins with a vowel sound, you use *an*. And hey—one more thing. *A*, *an*, and *the* are also adjectives. We'll talk more about them later on.

You use *the* before a specific noun, and you can use it whether the noun is singular or plural. For example:

The computer (when you're talking about a specific one, like mine)
The keys to my house

YOUR TURN

In the following four sentences, label each noun common or proper and concrete or abstract. Remember to capitalize all proper nouns.

1. She doesn't like to admit it to most people, but rosita has a huge collection of stuffed animals from toys "r" us.

2. I have lived in the town of paramus for my whole life.

3. My favorite television show, joan of arcadia, airs on friday nights.

4. My sister, marie, worships social studies and wants to be a cnn reporter, traveling to exotic countries like ethiopia and pakistan.

Turn the following five singular nouns into plural nouns.

5. phone ___________

6. knife ___________

7. kiss ___________

8. army ___________

9. alumnus ___________

* * * * *

I told Rosita we were just about done with the basics of nouns, and she was relieved to see that some grammar topics really aren't that tough. She was also thrilled for the excuse to take a break and check her email, so we switched my computer back on and I waited for her to log on to her account for the millionth time that night.

"Oh, my God!" Rosita squealed a moment later.

My heart jumped. I knew what that squeal meant. Was I an evil person for not wanting Rosita and Charlie to end up together? I knew I should be happy for her, but I couldn't help feeling a major twinge of hurt.

"What'd he say?" I asked, forcing myself to sound as excited as possible.

"Here, read it," she instructed, jumping up from my desk chair so I could sit. Reluctantly, I plopped down in front of the screen and started to read Charlie's response.

Hey Rosita,

It was great meeting you, too. It seems like we do have a lot in common. And I was so psyched to get an email that I can actually read for once! You seem like a really smart girl, on top of being so nice.

Are you free next Saturday night?

--Charlie

I closed my eyes for a second, trying to push away the intense wave of jealousy coming over me.

"Did you see? He thinks I'm smart! Arianna, you're amazing," Rosita gushed. "But I can't let him down now. You have to help me write back!"

I sighed. "Okay," I said. "But can we do it tomorrow night? I'm really tired, and I have some homework to finish before school tomorrow."

"Yeah, that's fine. He waited a day to write back to me, so I should really wait until tomorrow anyway. Thanks again. You're the best!"

She grabbed me for a quick hug, then practically danced out of my room and down the stairs.

I was in deep here, and I wasn't sure how I was going to get out.

3

CHAPTER 3
THE PRONOUN

Before I knew it, it was Monday afternoon and Rosita was back at my place. We were getting ready to compose a reply to Charlie's email.

"It has to be perfect," Rosita said, as if it was the first time she'd made this opinion known.

"Rosi, he obviously likes you," I said. "I'm not sure why he keeps using that bat emoticon, but I think you're fine to do this on your own."

"No, I can't—he specifically said I seem *smart*, remember? And that's all because of you! You're the one he really thinks is smart, Arianna."

As if I could forget that. As if I hadn't been wondering all day, in the back of my mind, whether I could have been the girl Charlie liked if I'd had the guts to start talking to him back when we were in school together.

"Come on, you know you're happy finally getting the chance to teach me all this grammar, anyway," she teased, her dark brown eyes gleaming.

I sighed. "Okay, fine. Let's get started."

We sat in front of the computer, and Rosita dictated the message she wanted me to write. But I kept finding myself getting into serious pronoun trouble as I typed. It was really confusing trying to write an email that was supposed to be from Rosita when I wasn't actually her, especially because so many of the things she wanted to say were things that I, Arianna, felt as well! The "I, you, we" thing was really getting to me. In fact, this whole situation was turning into a giant mess.

After about half an hour, we finally produced an email that satisfied both of us, and I had a massive headache. I decided the time had come for something that always cheered me up, as strange as it might seem to some people: more grammar talk.

WHAT PRONOUNS ARE

If you look at the word *pronoun*, you can get a quick and easy clue about what a pronoun is—yep, the word *noun* is stuck right in there! A **pronoun** is a word that can take the place of a noun in a sentence. Usually the pronoun is subbing for a specific noun that came up earlier in the sentence or in the sentence or two before it. But some pronouns operate in slightly more mysterious ways. Aren't you dying to find out how? Read on!

PERSONAL PRONOUNS

Charlie is really funny and nice. Charlie is also hot. I'd like to spend a lot of time hanging out with Charlie.

Somebody slap me. Not only are those sentences outright betrayals of my friendship with Rosita, but I seem to have a problem repeating Charlie's name incessantly. Since getting Charlie out of my head isn't going to happen any time soon, the least I can do is try to stop saying his name so much. I need to replace his name with something else so I sound a little less crazy. Here I go again:

Charlie is really funny and nice. He is also hot. I'd like to spend a lot of time hanging out with him.

I'm still a bad friend . . . but at least I sound less like a parrot, squawking Charlie's name over and over again. Thank goodness for our good friends the *pronouns*, which, as you've seen firsthand, take the place of nouns in a sentence.

You use pronouns all the time to refer to specific people and things. The most common pronouns are:

I	me	her	she
you	we	it	them
he	him	they	

These are **personal pronouns**. Check out the personal pronouns in these sentences (they're in italics!):

> If Rosita and Charlie end up together, *I* am going to lose my mind. Why couldn't *she* have met someone else? Who am *I* kidding—*he* is already hers. Stuff like this always happens to *me*.

To understand which pronoun to use when, you have to understand what point of view the writing takes. This point of view, by the way, is called **person**. Each personal pronoun links up with a particular point of view. There are three different kinds:

FIRST PERSON

Take this book, for example: I'm telling my story from the point of view of the writer, me, Arianna, so I use the pronouns *I* and *me* to tell you so. When I talk about myself and Rosita, I use *we* and *us*. Talking to you like I'm doing now, I'm using what's called the **first person**. *I*, *me*, *we*, and *us* are first-person pronouns.

SECOND PERSON

I've also been addressing you, the reader, by using the pronoun *you*. When I address you, I'm using the **second person**. The sentence *These are probably the pronouns you use most often* is in the second person, and—tada!—there's the personal pronoun associated with the second person, *you*, right there in the sentence. Any sentence that addresses you, the reader, as if we were talking together is in the second person.

THIRD PERSON

When I'm describing things from a distance—like if I talk about what Charlie and Rosita did on their date—I use the pronouns *it, he, she, they, them, her*, and *him*. This is called—you guessed it!—the **third-person** point of view. It ignores the person doing the writing and the person reading the writing, and focuses on who or what the writing is about. *Rosita likes Charlie. He's lucky to have her.*

REFLEXIVE AND RECIPROCAL PRONOUNS

Being selfish is okay sometimes, especially if you're one of these pronouns:

myself	yourself	himself
herself	itself	oneself
themselves	ourselves	yourselves

To see how they're used, take a look at some of my obsessive, persistent thoughts:

If Rosita and Charlie end up with *each other*, she's going to drive *herself* crazy trying to learn about grammar, and I'm going to lose *myself* in jealousy. Rosita hates grammar, but I love it. Charlie and I are perfect for *one another*! Charlie and Rosita need to see the truth for *themselves*!

Herself, *myself*, and *themselves* reflect nouns in the sentence: *Rosita*, *I*, and *Charlie and Rosita*. These are called **reflexive pronouns**, since, like I just said, they reflect the nouns they stand in for. Reflexive pronouns all end with *-self* or *-selves*, so they're easy to spot.

You probably noticed that I skipped over two of the italicized pronouns in the passage: *each other* and *one another*. It takes two to tango . . . and these pronouns stand in for two nouns. Think of it this way: Let's say Charlie gets Rosita a gift, and she gives one back—she reciprocates. They're both happy now that they've given gifts to *each other*. No surprise here: Pronouns like *each other* and *one another* are called **reciprocal pronouns**.

DEMONSTRATIVE PRONOUNS

Picture one of those pointers teachers use to indicate a location on a classroom map. Like pointers, some pronouns point to or identify specific nouns. There are only a handful:

this	that	these	those

They're pretty important. Check this out:

"Do you want to borrow *this* CD?" Rosita asked.
"No—*that* one," I said.

I'll italicize more pointer pronouns in more of my obsessive, unfriendly thoughts:

This crush of mine has got to end. If I liked someone, Rosita wouldn't try to steal him for herself. Or would she? . . . No! I'm sounding crazier and crazier. *That* idea sounds like the plot of a bad teen movie. Stuff like *this* always goes through my mind. Maybe I should be in Hollywood!

Since these pronouns demonstrate something exactly like a teacher with a pointer would, we call them **demonstrative pronouns**. They can act like nouns or adjectives, depending on how they're used.

NOUN: Stuff like *this* always goes through my mind.
ADJECTIVE: *This* crush of mine has got to end.

INDEFINITE PRONOUNS

The pronouns we've seen so far always stand in for a noun in the sentence, or they emphasize one of those nouns. But some pronouns keep you guessing—like the cliff-hanger endings of soap operas on Fridays. Sometimes you might see a pronoun, but you won't know whom or what it refers to. Look at an example:

If Rosita and Charlie end up together, I am going to lose my mind. Why couldn't she have met *someone* else?

That *someone* is maddeningly vague, isn't it? If we knew who that *someone* was, a lot of problems would be solved! I sure don't have anyone specific in mind . . . as long as it's not Charlie.

The pronouns that hide their identities are:

someone	all	anyone
both	either	everything
nobody	many	some

Since we can't be definite about who or what these pronouns refer to, we call them **indefinite pronouns**.

BE SPECIFIC

Use indefinite pronouns cautiously. If people don't know what you're talking about, they're not going to care what you say! If you have *something* specific in mind, you'll avoid words like *something*.

AGREEMENT

Pronouns and the words they replace have a fairy-tale relationship: They never disagree. At least, they shouldn't, if your sentence is in working order. You should always make sure the pronoun matches its noun in all the important ways: *person* (first, second, or third), *number* (singular or plural), and *gender* (guy or girl).

Here's an example of one sentence where the agreement isn't happening:

WRONG: The *guy* at the game gave me *their* number.

Why is this wrong? Let's ignore the fact that I've never met a guy at a game, since this is purely an example sentence. No, the real problem is that *their* is a pronoun subbing for *guy*, but *guy* is singular and *their* is plural.

RIGHT: The *guy* at the game gave me *his* number.

Notice that *his* also matches up with *guy* in person (both third) and gender (both male).

DOUBLE TROUBLE

Sometimes a pronoun replaces two nouns. Look at what happens when I talk about Charlie and one of his cute friends without using any pronouns:

Charlie and his friend are funny. Charlie and his friend make me laugh, and I like Charlie and his friend a lot.

Wow. That's really annoying. We definitely need a pronoun to come to the rescue! How do we know which one? Well, we need to look at the word that joins those nouns together: *and*. Nouns joined by *and* usually take plural pronouns:

Charlie and his friend are funny. They make me laugh, and I like them a lot.

Much better! I used the plural pronouns *they* and *them* to replace *Charlie and his friend*. Here's another example:

The guy playing sax and the guy playing drums gave me *their* numbers.

Never mind that this sentence has left reality far behind. Just notice the plural pronoun *their*, because I'm about to leave reality even further behind with my next example. When two nouns follow *each* or *every*, use a singular pronoun:

Every saxophonist and drummer gave me *his* number.

Ha! I'm having a fun fantasy moment here, but hold on a second. What if some of the sax players and drummers are female? Don't automatically use *his*. Instead, use *his* or *her*:

Every saxophonist and drummer gave me *his* or *her* number.

You could also rewrite the sentence so that the subject is plural. Then the pronoun will be plural, too, and you'll avoid having to use two gender-specific ones:

The *saxophonists and drummers* gave me *their* numbers.

In very rare instances, you could have a noun that looks like two people but isn't actually. Say the same guy played both sax and drums in the band. (Boy, I'd like to meet *him*!) You'd use the singular *his* (or *her*, for a multitalented girl) to let your reader know that you're naming two features of only one person:

The *saxophonist and drummer* gave me *his* number.

Now let's look at another way to use compound nouns, with *or* or *nor*. Make the pronoun agree with whichever noun is closer:

Neither the *coach* nor the *team members*
gave me *their* numbers.

Ah, back to reality. *Team members* is plural, so I've used *their*. Let's try it the other way around:

Neither the *team members* nor the *coach* gave me *his* number.

Okay, I made the pronoun *his* agree with the nearer noun, *coach*, but it sounds weird. In general, when one subject is plural and the other one is singular, put the singular one first. This strategy will make your sentences sound better.

Here's another good reason to follow that strategy: What if the coach is female? Remember, I didn't actually go to this football game, so I shouldn't assume that the coach is male. *His* or *her* is a better choice when it comes to nouns like *coach, teacher, astronaut,* or any other noun that doesn't have a gender built into it.

PRONOUN PILEUPS

Don't explode or anything, but consider this: What if the noun a pronoun replaces is itself a pronoun, an indefinite pronoun like *anybody, everyone, many*, or *something*? As you know, indefinite pronouns don't refer to specific people or things, so how are you supposed to know whether they're singular or plural, male or female?

The answer, sadly, is that you can't know for sure, and now you really know why they're called indefinite pronouns! The good news is that most indefinite pronouns are singular, even *everybody, everything,* and *much*. You can memorize the few that aren't: *both, few, many,* and *several*. The bad news is that, since indefinite pronouns don't tell you which gender they are, you'll occasionally be tempted to cheat and use the plural pronouns *they, them,* or *their* to replace them.

WRONG: *Everyone* at the game gave me *their* number.

I'm back in fantasyland with my example, I know. I had to escape from all that bad news. Unfortunately, I did not escape from bad grammar. Here, this one's better:

RIGHT: *Everyone* at the game gave me *his or her* number.

It sounds a little awkward, but the pronoun and the noun it replaces agree.

GOOD GUESSES

Sometimes the way that an indefinite pronoun is used will tell you its gender. Let's say I know for a fact that River Dell's football team is all male. I could write this:

Everyone on River Dell's football team gave me *his* number.

Indefinite pronouns aren't the only parts of speech being vague about their gender. Generic nouns like *person* or *individual* play the same game. Once again, if the gender of the noun is clear, you can use *he*, *his*, and *him* or *she*, *hers*, and *her*. If the gender isn't clear, don't guess, and don't cheat by using *they*, *their*, or *them*. Use a pronoun from both genders:

No *person* at the game gave me *his* or *her* number.

There's absolutely, positively no way to tell whether *person* is a boy or a girl. You'll either live with *his* or *her*, or rewrite the sentence, possibly using the plural noun *people* instead of person:

At the game, no *people* gave me *their* numbers.

COLLECTIVE NOUNS

Some nouns, like *family* or *crowd*, suggest a lot of people without being plural. They're called **collective nouns**, and they might tempt you to use the pronouns *they*, *their*, or *them* to replace them. But don't do it—unless it's clear from the sentence that the members of the group are acting individually:

The *team* gave *their* numbers out to everybody.

Every team member has his own phone number, which means that they act individually when they hand their numbers out.

If the members of the group are acting as one, pair the collective noun with a third-person singular pronoun:

The *team* traveled to away games on *its* own private bus.

Each member of the team doesn't have a private bus . . . but wouldn't it be cool if they did?

KEEP IT CLEAR

Pronouns and the nouns they replace are so big on agreeing that they also like to hang close in sentences. Okay, actually, they're just parts of speech and they don't have feelings. But if they *did*, they'd be as tight as Rosita and I are, because they sort of have to be. A pronoun not tied clearly enough to its noun can cause big-time confusion. Always make sure that someone reading your sentence without any idea whom or what you're talking about can easily identify the noun the pronoun replaces.

Try figuring this sentence out, for instance:

If I'd gone to the game against River Dell, I could have talked to Charlie and Rich, and maybe I'd be going out with *him*.

You all know which "him" I mean, since I've pretty much made myself an open book to you—literally! But what if some stranger read that sentence? That person wouldn't know if I meant Charlie or Rich. In this example, it's better not to use a pronoun at all. (There's enough Charlie-related confusion already!)

As you know, pronouns can have different jobs in a sentence. And depending on the jobs they do, they can take on different forms. For example, you can't switch around *she* and *her*—you need each one at different times. The form of a pronoun is called its **case**, and the case depends on what the pronoun's job is in the sentence. There are three possible cases.

POSSESSIVE CASE

Remember the possessive nouns we used to identify whose stuff was cluttering up my room? Well, we can use pronouns the same way. Instead of saying the fabulous Toasters CD is Rosita's, we can say it's *hers*. Possessive pronouns show ownership just like possessive nouns do. Some examples of possessive pronouns are *my, our, your, her, hers, his, its, their, mine, ours,* and *theirs.*

Take a look at these sentences. The possessive pronouns are in italics:

All of this deception is going to make me lose *my* mind. Besides, emails don't really matter anymore—he's already *hers*. *His* heart belongs to Rosita now.

Notice how *my* comes before *mind*, but *hers* is all by itself. A possessive pronoun can come in two forms: *adjective* or *noun*. It's in the adjective form when it's next to the noun it explains, like how *my* tells you whose mind is going to be lost (as if there's any question here!). *Hers* is in the noun form, because it's got that *s*, which allows it to stand there all by itself substituting for the possessive noun *Rosita's*.

SUBJECTIVE CASE

A pronoun, like any noun, can serve as the subject of a sentence or of a clause within a sentence. Remember, the subject is the person or thing who's performing the action of the verb. For instance:

She exudes so much confidence.
I wrote the email, even though *she* has so much confidence.

OBJECTIVE CASE

A pronoun can also act as an object in the sentence. In other words, instead of performing the action of the verb, it is being acted upon.

Sometimes, I'm really jealous of *her*.
I wish Charlie could have liked *me*.

SUBJECTIVE CASE VS. OBJECTIVE CASE

One of the most common grammar mistakes people make is mixing up these cases, especially with *who* or *whom* and *I* or *me*.

WHO/WHOM

The key to remember is that *who* and *I* are subjective-case pronouns, and *whom* and *me* are objective-case pronouns. That means you use *who* or *I* to fill in for a subject, and *whom* or *me* to fill in for the objects anywhere else in the sentence.

WRONG: *Who* does Charlie like?

Who is misused because Charlie is the subject of that sentence. The question is asking about Charlie's feelings. The person Charlie likes is the object of the sentence. So the right way to do it is:

RIGHT: *Whom* does Charlie like?

If you're looking for a sentence that uses who, not whom, think of one that needs a subject pronoun, like:

Who likes Charlie?

I/ME

WRONG: *Me* and Rosita have a crush on the same guy.

So what's up with that? Yeah, I know, it's *wrong* in the whole "you shouldn't like your best friend's crush" way, but it's also just plain wrong. *Me* is part of the subject of the sentence–the people who are having the crush. If someone else were having a crush on *us*, then *Rosita and me* would move into the object slot, after the preposition *on*.

RIGHT: Rosita and *I* have a crush on the same guy.
RIGHT: Someone has a crush on Rosita and *me*.

GET THE ORDER RIGHT

When *I* is grouped with someone or something else, as in that example above, you always use *I* last in the group. The same goes for *me*.

YOUR TURN

In the following five sentences, fill in the blanks with the correct pronouns, then underline all of the other pronouns.

1. My friends Sonya and Kaitlin like to ask for my help with ______ (*their*, *hers*, *his*) English homework.

2. Between you and ______(*I*, *me*), they don't really need help, but ______(*who*, *whom*) would I spend fourth period with if not ______(*they*, *them*)?

3. Today, Sonya said, "Kat and ______(*I*, *me*) will never catch up with your English crowd, even though ______(*they*, *it*, *he*, or *she*) moves pretty slowly!"

4. I shot back, "Every science nerd I know has to tell ______(*their*, *his*, *its*, *his*, or *her*) little English nerd joke, even though jokes about science nerds are far more common than ones about ______ (*we*, *us*) English types!"

5. Neither Sonya nor her science-nerd friends have made ______(*her*, *their*, *his*, or *her*) English nerd jokes funny enough for anyone else to remember, much less laugh, so I can't tell you any of ______(*they*, *them*).

Fix the following five sentences so that the pronouns and the nouns they replace match.

6. Everyone in fourth period has their own opinion about Sonya's jokes, which strike only she as hilarious.

7. It seems obvious that me and her have wildly different ideas of funny, but when a Chemistry quiz is staring ourselves in the face, nobody is laughing their head off, not even Sonya.

8. Chemistry and English both have its good points, being interesting to I, challenging, and good preparation for college, but, as you probably guessed, the easiest courses are not them.

9. I guess I'd rather spend fourth period listening to Sonya's terrible jokes, each of us studying for whatever we have next, than spend it with a truly hilarious person who has their own friends and who we aren't truly friends with, either.

10. Much—maybe all—of her goofiness is actually lovable, when you consider Sonya as their good-hearted source, and though her taste in jokes may be dismal, her taste in friendship is fabulous.

* * * * *

Once we wrapped up the lesson on pronouns, Rosita insisted that we flip my computer back on and give her email a quick check before she went home.

Sure enough, Charlie had already written back. He hadn't wasted any time this go-around, and it seemed obvious that Rosita had snagged her guy, as always.

She let out a gasp after she finished the email. "Read it!"

I obliged, and saw (in between emoticons) that Charlie had officially asked her out on a date next Saturday, for a specific time and everything.

I just couldn't help wishing that the *you* he was addressing in his email were me. . . .

CHAPTER 4
THE VERB, PART I

Suddenly, my whole life had become focused on Rosita and Charlie's impending date. I mean, there we were in the computer lab on Wednesday during our media class, supposedly doing research on the Internet, while, instead, Rosita and Charlie were sending each other instant messages to decide what to do on Saturday night.

You would think I wouldn't have been involved in such gritty details, right? Well, guess again. Rosita was now petrified to type a word without me at her side, so I was huddled next to her, helping her shape every little sentence she wrote to Charlie.

"He wants to know if there are any movies I want to see," she said aloud, as if I hadn't seen the words on the screen myself.

"Right," I said.

"So?" She stared at me expectantly.

What, was I supposed to read her mind now or something? "So, *are* there?" I asked. "Any movies you want to see, I mean?"

It was amazing. I'd never seen my confident, outgoing best friend so paralyzed with fear that she'd scare the guy away. She really, really liked him.

"I don't know. What do you think would make me sound smart? What do *you* want to see right now?"

"Rosita, this is crazy!"

"Shh," she hissed, glancing behind me at our teacher, Mr. Wilkinson. Luckily, everyone else in the room was also chattering away, since we were doing the assignment in pairs. He hadn't seemed to notice that our conversation had little to do with whether the upcoming advances in technology would "shift the paradigm of mainstream news" or not.

"Rosi, I can't tell you what movies you want to see," I said, lowering my voice. "Oh, wait. He just sent you something else. See, you waited so long to respond that he probably thinks you're not into the movie idea. He's got a couple of suggestions here. Do you want to '**go out to dinner, go mini-golfing, or check out** the newly added arcade games at Dave & Buster's in the Palisades Park mall?'"

Rosita stared back at me, a deep frown creasing her face. "I don't know," she said. "Too many choices. Come on, just tell me what to say."

"Fine," I said, "I will, if it'll get this over with already." I leaned over the computer and typed, "What if we check out Dave & Buster's and then eat dinner afterward at one of the restaurants in the mall?"

"There," I said. "All done. Who would've guessed that I'm the shy one?"

"Yeah, well, I'm only shy in email," Rosita complained. "In person, I know I'll be fine, as long as you keep prepping me on this grammar stuff."

"Okay," I said. "I guess it's time for verbs. We'll work on them after school today."

WHAT VERBS ARE

Want to know what's going on? Then you'll need a verb. **Verbs** are the parts of sentences that show *action* or, less thrillingly but just as important, *being*. Want that in plain English?

ACTION VERBS

For a sentence to be a sentence, people, places, things, or ideas must act in some way. What the nouns do can be physical or mental. Here are a couple of examples:

My sister and I *eat* pizza regularly.
Rosita *thinks* about grammar a lot these days. I *wonder* why?

When an action is taking place—like when someone is eating or thinking or wondering—the verb is called an **action verb**.

LINKING VERBS

Sometimes, a verb doesn't express an action. Like in this sentence:

Rosita *is* the confident one.

The verb *is* links the two parts of the sentence together, but Rosita isn't *doing* anything. She's not performing an activity. Instead, she's *being* something—the confident one. When a verb expresses being, it's called a **linking verb**. Linking verbs are like equal signs in math. They connect the subject of a sentence (like *Rosita*) and another part of speech.

The most common linking verbs are forms of *to be*, but here's one more:

Rosita *seems* bored.

Again, the linking verb connects Rosita to what she's being, but notice that this time she's connected to an adjective, *bored*, instead of a noun, like *one* in the sentence above.

HELPING VERBS

Some verbs don't show action or being. Instead, they help other verbs shift into certain tenses, like the future tense, perfect tense, or progressive tense. (Don't get tense. We're getting to tenses!) Verbs that help other verbs are called—I'm not kidding—**helping verbs**.

One of the most common helping verbs is, again, *be*, but *had, will, could*, and *might* are some others. Look for a helping verb to be just in front of a main verb, practically holding its hand. For example:

I *had* helped Rosita with boy problems in the past.
Charlie *will* like the email—I'm sure of it.

Verbs are shady characters sometimes, and sometimes they like to dress up and act like nouns. Look at this example:

Falling in love is a great experience.

You might think *falling in love* expresses an action, since, after all, you know full well that *fall* is a verb. But look closely: There's an *-ing* on the end of that verb. Hold on—that verb is acting like a noun! It's the subject of the sentence! The action of falling has become a thing! The main verb in the sentence, then, is *is*.

Here's another example where the verb is acting like a noun:

Meeting an incredible guy means you win the football game, even when your team loses.

Here the main verb of the sentence is *means*, and the subject doing the action is the phrase *meeting an incredible guy*.

Verbs are two-timers, aren't they? The good news is you can tell when they're cheating at their *real* job because they only do it when they end in *-ing* or *-ed*. Verbs that end this way are in the **participle** form.

One more trick verbs like to use:

To meet a guy is my goal.

When verbs are in full regalia like this—when that little *to* dresses them up—they're in the **infinitive** form. They can be nouns then, too.

VERB TENSE

When does the action in a sentence take place? You look to the verb in a sentence to find out. The *when* aspect of a verb is called **tense**. Did it already happen? Is it happening now? Is it going to happen tomorrow? Aren't you dying to find out?

SIMPLE TENSES

The three easiest tenses are the basics: *present*, *past*, and *future*.

SIMPLE PRESENT

An action that's happening in the present, or something that happens regularly, is in the **simple present** tense. Simple present verbs are just the base form of a verb, like this:

As I *type* an email, I *realize* that I always *type* all of my emails.

THE *S* EXCEPTION

For all the regular verbs that follow the rule above, there's one exception for simple present tense. When the verb is matched with a third-person singular subject, either a noun or the pronouns *he, she*, and *it*, the verb takes an extra -*s* or -*es* at the end. So:

As *Rosita* types an email, *she* realizes that *she* rarely types anything!

SIMPLE PAST

Actions that happened in the past and don't come into the present are in the **simple past** tense. For this tense, you usually add a -*d* or -*ed* to the end of the verb:

I *typed* an email yesterday and *realized*
that I always *type* all of my emails.

Notice how *type* in the last clause stays in the present tense, because I continue typing to this very day!

SIMPLE FUTURE

An action that hasn't happened yet, but will happen in the future, is in the **simple future** tense. In fact, you actually put the word *will* (our first helping verb!) in front of the base form of the verb to make it future tense:

I *will type* an email again soon, no doubt.

PERFECT TENSES

Okay, we've left the simple tense behind, and unfortunately the other ones aren't called anything like "easy tense" or "cakewalk tense." Perfect tense is a little tougher, but it's still doable. You use the **perfect** tense whenever you're talking about an ongoing action that has a *definite ending*. Why would you be talking about such an action? Usually the timing of the ended action relates to some other action, which is also in the sentence. The perfect tense comes in handy to describe what you were doing when you were interrupted, or your life changed, or you got that fateful email. . . .

To make it, you'll need another helping verb in addition to *will*: the verb *have*. Here's the deal.

PRESENT PERFECT

The **present perfect** tense shows an action that began in the past but has just been completed right here and now. It's an exception to the other perfect tenses, because it's not as suggestive of an interrupting action:

Rosita *has listened* carefully to my every word.

PAST PERFECT

The **past perfect** tense expresses an action that was over and done with before another action took place. As in this sentence, the past perfect requires two actions to justify its use:

Rosita *had listened* carefully, until she tuned me out.

Notice how the interrupting action of tuning me out is in the simple past tense. Only the action that had continued up to the interruption should be in the past perfect tense.

FUTURE PERFECT

Interested in hearing about the future perfect tense? Yeah, I know you are. You may be wondering how a tense that shows something that hasn't even happened yet could also show a definite ending in sight. The answer is: The **future perfect** tense clues you in to something you know will end in the future. Check it out:

Rosita *will have listened* to every word I say by the time she leaves this room.

Just like the past perfect, the future perfect tense needs two actions. Its interrupting action also takes a different tense from the future perfect: the simple present. Weird, huh?

IS IT OVER?

Remember, only the present perfect tense can get away with not having an interrupting or terminating action.

PROGRESSIVE TENSES

Hey, we're making *progress*—we're already at the *progressive* tense! (Sorry, that was bad, I know.)

The **progressive** tense helps you show that an action is going on for some period of time. When is all this happening? That depends on if it's present progressive, past progressive, or future progressive.

PRESENT PROGRESSIVE

When the subject of a sentence is performing the action in the present without stopping, the verb is in the present progressive tense. A fast and easy hint that you're looking at the progressive tense is when you see the helping verb *be* and the letters *-ing* stuck onto the base form of the verb. A verb ending in *-ing* is called a **present participle**. Here come a helping verb and participle now:

I *am talking* about grammar.

PAST PROGRESSIVE

Even though past tense is used for actions that are over in the present, you can still have a **past progressive** tense to describe an action that continued for a while back when it *did* happen. For example:

According to Rosita, I *was talking* about grammar for a long time.

FUTURE PROGRESSIVE

The **future progressive** tense helps you express an action that's already gotten started and is going to continue into the future. As with all future tenses, you'll need that helping verb *will*:

I *will be talking* about grammar until Rosita begs me to stop.

TO BE (OR MAYBE NOT)

To make things even more interesting, there are always irregular verbs. (What? You don't think this stuff is interesting? Okay, fine, maybe it's just me . . . .) The most common irregular verb is *be*, which you're probably getting used to by now in its various forms, *am, is, are, was, were, be, been,* and *being*. You've probably noticed that it pops up in different forms depending on which person and number its subject is: first, second, or third, in singular or plural. And now surely you suspect that it changes according to which *tense* it's expressing. The process of changing a verb's form to match person, number, and tense is called **conjugation**.

Let's conjugate the verb *to be*, starting with the person of its subject:

- If the subject is first-person singular: I *am* an irregular verb.
- If the subject is first-person plural: We *are* irregular verbs.
- If the subject is second-person singular/plural: You *are* an irregular verb.
- If the subject is third-person singular: He/She/It *is* an irregular verb.
- If the subject is third-person plural: They *are* is an irregular verb.

Notice how the first-person, second-person, and third-person plural all get the same version, *are*.

Here's how it works in the past tense:

- I, he, she, or it *was* an irregular verb.
- We, you, or they *were* irregular verbs.

AVOID BEING

Okay, I don't mean you shouldn't *be* or anything. I just mean you should try not to use the word *be* if you want your writing to sizzle. Find stronger, more active verbs to use instead. Which of these sentences tells you more?

Charlie *is* with Rosita.
Charlie *dates* Rosita.

Even as a helping verb to make the progressive tense, *be* only waters things down:

Charlie *is dating* Rosita.

This sentence, while grammatically correct, just doesn't have the flash of the sentence *Charlie dates Rosita*.

YOUR TURN

For each of these sentences, provide the indicated form of the verb.

1. Rosita and my friendship (*persevere*, present perfect) through thick and thin.

2. Until I (*meet*, simple past) her, I (*have*, past perfect) no genuine best friend.

3. I (*think*, simple past) I (*know*, simple past) what (*make*, simple past) a friendship, but I (*kid*, past progressive) myself.

4. One of my friends from middle school, Lena, (*cheer*, simple past) me up after I (*bomb*, past perfect) a quiz, for example, and I (*do*, simple past) the same when her gerbil (*die*, past progressive), but I never (*spend*, simple past) the kind of time with Lena that Rosita and I (*spend*, simple present) together.

5. By next June, I (*be*, future perfect) friends with Rosita for three years.

6. We (*go*, present progressive) strong.

7. Since you (*follow*, present perfect) my story so avidly, you (*know*, simple present) how great Rosita (*be*, simple present).

8. Now I (*use*, present progressive) the word *friend* more carefully.

9. Don't (*forget*, simple present) to pass on any great boyfriend-getting ideas you (*happen*, simple present) to have.

10. I (*need*, simple future) them, as you (*see*, future perfect) by the time you finish this book!

* * * * *

I spent the rest of the week listening to Rosita blather on about her date with Charlie and trying super-hard not to go crazy with jealousy. Then, on Friday afternoon, there was a sudden twist.

Rosita called me up and said she needed a huge favor. I started to tell her that I refused to use one of those crazy devices where I'd feed her words on her date, but she just cracked up laughing and said not to worry, that wasn't it.

"What do you need, then?" I asked.

"Here's the thing. See, Charlie totally forgot that he promised his friend Theo they'd go to Dave & Buster's together sometime soon. Theo doesn't have a license yet, and I guess he's dying to see those new games. Charlie feels kind of bad and wants to bring Theo, but he doesn't want to postpone our date, either. So, he was wondering if I could bring a friend along for Theo. I thought maybe you'd want to come."

Talk about rubbing salt into a wound. I was going to have a front-row view of Rosita's first date with the guy of my dreams, Charlie Houston. But how could I say no? I was always talking about how I wished I could meet more guys, and there was no good excuse for not wanting to help Rosita.

"Okay," I agreed. "I'll be there." What was I getting myself into?

5

CHAPTER 5
THE VERB, PART II

"Arianna, I can't believe you didn't tell me you knew Charlie!"

I stared across the table at Rosita and Charlie, who were huddled together under Charlie's black satin cape, and shifted awkwardly in my seat. "It just, uh, didn't seem important," I mumbled. "I mean, we didn't really *know* each other."

"Yeah, I barely remember her at all," Charlie said with an easy smile that stabbed a nice-size stake into my heart. "But there was something a little familiar about her, and then when you mentioned she went to Paramus, I realized we had to have gone to school together."

"Yep," I said. "We did." I glanced away, hoping Rosita would be too gaga over Charlie to notice that I was blushing.

"Small world," Theo chimed in from next to me. Wow, it was almost the first time I'd heard him speak.

The four of us were sitting in a booth at T.G.I. Friday's, waiting for our appetizers, after we'd wandered around Dave & Buster's for about an hour. Theo seemed nice enough, but kind of, well, boring. He just didn't say very much. Charlie, on the other hand, had been the life of the party, along with Rosita. The two of them had totally hit it off right in front of me, teasing each other as they played the arcade games and sharing stuff about themselves in between turns at the controls.

Why couldn't I be as comfortable with myself as Rosita was? It seemed so easy for her to talk to Charlie, when it had always seemed impossible to me.

"Ooh, our food's coming," Rosita said as the waiter walked up with one plate of nachos and another of potato skins. He dropped off the two appetizers at our table, along with individual plates for us to split everything up.

"So, how should we do this?" Charlie asked after the waiter was gone. He and I were sharing the potato skins, and Rosita and Theo were the ones who'd opted for nachos. But it was a little awkward with the way we were sitting. "Here, Arianna, why don't you give me your plate and I'll put some skins on it? I'm glad you were up for splitting them. They're my favorite appetizer here."

"Yeah, mine too," I said softly.

God, couldn't the universe realize how wrong this all was and just switch my place with Rosita's? I knew I belonged with Charlie. Of course, I could also see that Rosita really liked him, and then I felt even worse.

I needed a distraction, I realized as I chewed away at my cheesy potato skins. I decided to do a mental review of the rest of my verb lesson for Rosita.

SUBJECT/VERB AGREEMENT

You might have noticed that agreement is a pretty big theme in grammar. When you're putting together a sentence, it's really important to make sure all the different parts agree. That's true for verbs, too. Verbs need to agree with their subjects, and agreement doesn't come easy, just like between me and my older sister, Marie. But when Marie and I do agree on something, our house is a much happier place to be, and when your verb agrees with the subject, ditto for the sentence.

AGREE BY NUMBER AND PERSON

Remember our old friends number and person? We always have to figure out whether to classify a subject as singular or plural and first, second, or third person, because subjects must agree with their verbs. The form of a verb changes depending on the subject's number and person.

For some reason, singular third-person subjects are very needy when you're talking in the present tense. You have to use a different verb form for them from the ones you use for everything else. So when you have a singular third-person subject, you add *-s* or *-es* to the end of the base form of the verb, like this:

Charlie *likes* potato skins.
Theo never *talks*.

DON'T BE DISTRACTED!

Sometimes the verb is separated from its subject by one or more words. It's not too confusing when it's just one word, like *never* in that sentence about Theo, and when that word isn't a noun. But sometimes you might get a sentence where there's another noun between the subject and the verb, like *That plate of nachos looks delicious.* Remember to use your detective skills to pick out the real subject, and if it's singular, like *plate*, then you add the -*s* to the verb even when there's another plural noun wedged in between that's connected to the subject.

SINGULAR OR PLURAL?

Sometimes it's tough to decide whether your subject is singular or plural. As I said above, sometimes other words wedge themselves between the subject and the verb, causing confusion. Here are some other tricky situations, so you'll be able to sail through them from now on, no problem.

COMPOUND SUBJECTS

What about when the actual subject of your sentence really is more than one person, place, or thing? The nouns are compounded (remember that word?), usually joined together by that neat little word *and*. Most of the time, compounded nouns count as a plural subject, so you use the verb form that matches a plural subject, as in this example:

The waiter and hostess here *look* very stressed.

Even though the waiter and hostess are third-person singular subjects by themselves, in this sentence we're sticking them together, so they become a plural subject.

JOINING PHRASES

Sometimes a subject looks compounded when it isn't. Phrases other than *and* that also join nouns together (*as well as*, *along with*, *in addition to*) might fool you into thinking you have a plural subject. Check it out:

Rosita, along with Theo, *likes* nachos.

Arianna, as well as Charlie, *works* hard in English.

Doesn't it seem like the verbs *like* and *work* should be third-person plural since the sentences talk about two people? Yeah, but remember: In grammar, things aren't always what they seem! Think of that phrase as a little extra added to the sentence, like salt sprinkled on some potato skins that are already complete by themselves. The subject of the original sentence is still third-person singular—*Rosita* in one case, and *Arianna*, in the other—so the verb has to have that *-s*.

EACH AND EVERY

Here we go again with the special cases. When you have more than one subject joined together with *and*, you use a *singular* verb form when the words *each* or *every* come before the subjects, like this:

Every waiter and waitress here *looks* stressed.

We can see the stress on each of their faces individually.

OR AND NOR

They sound like the names of two cartoon monsters, don't they? Anyway, some compound subjects are formed with the word pairs *either . . . or* and *neither . . . nor*, like this one:

Neither the hostess *nor* the waiters

When it's time to make whole sentences out of these kinds of subjects, you just have to make sure the verb agrees with whichever part of the subject it's closest to. If that part is singular, then you use a singular form of the verb. If it's plural you use the plural form. See how it works:

Neither the hostess nor the waiters *seem* to like working here.
Neither the waiters nor the hostess *seems* to like working here.

You could also have two or more nouns joined by *or* without *either*. The same principle applies: Make your verb agree with what's closest.

COLLECTIVE NOUNS

Collective nouns talk about a whole group as one thing, like *family*, *team*, or *class*. They sound singular, but they can actually be either singular or plural, depending on how they're being used in a sentence. Are they describing the whole unit as one thing, or are they referring to all the parts of the combined unit? You have to figure this out before you can decide what form of verb to pair up with the noun. Here are two examples:

The football team *disagree* about whether they want new uniforms.
The football team *disagrees* with the ref about that call.

In the first example, you're talking about the members of the team as a group of people who are disagreeing with each other, so that makes the word *team* a plural subject—which means you use the third-person plural form of the verb.

In the second sentence, the team is acting as one unit (just what Coach Brady would want, since he's always yelling, "There's no *I* in team, people!"). That means you use—you guessed it—the third-person singular form of the verb.

TITLES

Here's an easy rule for you: When the title of a book, movie, or TV show is the subject of a sentence, you always use the singular form of the verb:

Of Mice and Men tells a sad story.

CHANGING PLACES

Usually verbs come after subjects in the sentence. But what about those times when they switch spots? Again, you have to be extra careful to pinpoint the real subject of the sentence, wherever it is, and make sure the verb agrees. Here's one that could trip you up:

WRONG: Beside the nachos *sit* the plate of potato skins.
RIGHT: Beside the nachos *sits* the plate of potato skins.

The noun *nachos* is plural, so at first you might think the verb *sit* should be in the plural form. But the catch is, the nachos aren't the subject, even though they come first in the sentence. *Beside the nachos* (a prepositional phrase, by the way—we'll get to these) is just a description of where the real subject of the sentence—the *plate* (singular) of potato skins—can be found.

ACTIVE AND PASSIVE VOICE

Ever have a day where you just can't seem to get moving, when you'd be perfectly happy to just stay in bed and not do anything? Verbs have days like that as well. They can be strong and active, but they can also be weak and passive—that is, they can have either an **active voice** or **passive voice**. Yep, even though they're called "action verbs," they can have their lazy, passive days, too. Here's the skinny on the difference between active and passive voice.

ACTIVE VOICE

A sentence with a verb in the active voice shows the subject of the sentence acting, like this:

Charlie asked Rosita out for Saturday night.

Charlie's the subject, and the sentence shows him taking action—he asked Rosita out. No hinting around for Charlie—he just does what he needs to do!

PASSIVE VOICE

When a verb is in the passive voice, the subject of the sentence is being acted upon instead of acting:

Rosita was asked out by Charlie for Saturday night.

This time Rosita is the subject of the sentence, but we're hearing about something that happened to her—she was asked out—instead of hearing about something she did. She was just sitting back, maybe checking her email, and Charlie was the one who took action.

ACTIVE OR PASSIVE?

So, you're probably wondering what the big deal is. Why does it matter if the verb is active or passive? And, okay, if it *does* matter, when should you use one or the other?

Here's a rule of thumb: *You should almost always use the active voice.* Why?

Look at those two example sentences. The active one is stronger, less wordy, and less clunky. It gets right to the point with no confusion, and it keeps your subject in the control seat of the sentence. No wishy-washy subjects there! Don't let your subjects be lazy. Get them up off the couch, and make them act with strong, active verbs.

WHEN TO USE THE PASSIVE VOICE

You knew this was coming. . . . There are exceptions to every rule, and the *Use the active voice* rule is no exception! At certain times it makes sense to use the passive voice.

1. One reason to choose passive voice is when you don't know the "actor," or agent, of the sentence. Here's an example:

   The refrigerator door was left open last night.

   Maybe a soda bottle was sticking out too far—who knows? It doesn't matter. The door was left open, and now the milk is sour.
2. You can also use the passive voice when you know who the "actor" is, but you're trying to hide or downplay it to avoid responsibility (not that I'm advocating doing this or anything). For example, you could write:

   The homework didn't get done.

   Instead of:

   I didn't do the homework.

   Your teacher won't be fooled . . . but you might think it sounds less incriminating!
3. Sometimes the person or thing in your sentence that's receiving the action deserves more attention than the "actor" of the sentence, and the passive voice can help you shift the spotlight. Check out this line from our school newspaper article about Saturday's football game:

   The Paramus Spartans were defeated by River Dell, 42-10.

   If you go to Paramus High School, like me, then you care more about what happened to our team, the Spartans, than you do about the River Dell team.

YOUR TURN

In each of these sentences and clauses, underline the simple subject once and the verb it goes with twice. Insert the correct form of the verb if necessary.

1. Every appetizer and entrée at T.G.I. Friday's cost about the same.

2. Unlike some other restaurants I enjoy, here neither the onion rings nor the tostada are overpriced.

3. The staff definitely hates their jobs, though.

4. Rosita and Charlie, as well as Theo and me, try to be as nice as possible because the company of waiters keep shrinking and we don't have our nachos yet.

5. After all those potato skins and nachos come an ice-cream brownie, Death by Chocolate.

6. *Will and Grace* play on the TV behind the booth, and the Dixie Chicks blare on the jukebox.

7. Country, bluegrass, or swing music get my vote for most boring, and this date gets my vote for most awkward.

8. Are *awkward* and *boring* the right words for what I feel?

Rewrite the following sentences so that the verbs are in the active voice:

9. Although more surly service was risked, desserts were ordered by Rosita and me.

10. Nothing was said by Theo to suggest that a taste of my Death by Chocolate would be enjoyed.

* * * * *

It was a huge relief when the double date finally ended and I could curl up in bed at home, doing my best not to think too much about Charlie. It wasn't that I'd had a bad time. That was the problem, in fact. Charlie and Rosita were both so much fun to be around that I would have been having an excellent time if I'd been able to stop worrying about my own crush on my best friend's date.

I was pretty sure it had been as clear to Theo as it was to me that there was certainly no love connection between us. Too bad. It probably would have helped if I'd liked him. Then maybe I could have gotten over Charlie.

And maybe, just maybe, I could have stopped wondering if I were really the one who was right for Charlie. . . .

6

CHAPTER 6
ADJECTIVES AND ADVERBS

"You didn't even think he was cute?"

"He was okay," I acknowledged.

It was Sunday, and Rosita and I were in a familiar configuration in my room. She was stretched out on my bed, and I was sitting in my comfy desk chair, putting up with her inquisition about Theo. Apparently, this inquisition was a necessary part of the post-date analysis.

"He had good hair," I said, trying to throw her a bone.

"He had great hair! Yes! All thick and dark—just what you're always saying you like. So what's the problem?"

"Rosi, I'm not dating *hair* here. I just . . . I didn't think Theo was all that interesting. What's the big deal?"

"I don't know. I guess I wanted you to be as happy as I am," she said, "so I was hoping the you-and-Theo thing could happen."

Ouch. What a way to bring my guilt up a notch.

"So you really like Charlie, huh?"

"How could I not? He's amazing, don't you think? First of all, he's gorgeous. Plus he's really nice, he's funny, he's sweet when he talks about his little sister, he's incredibly smart—just like you—and he's a lot of fun. Even taking into consideration his cape and his black fingernail polish, I would say he's perfect, if I really believed there were a perfect guy."

I realized my nails were starting to dig into my skin and slowly unclenched my fist to flex my fingers.

"I guess our grammar work's all done, then? I mean, you and Charlie are all set, it seems."

"Are you kidding me? No way! I still have to write him a next-day email, saying I had a good time. I need to say how great last night was without sounding like some goopy idiot."

"Okay," I said halfheartedly. I was in so deep now, I didn't really see a way out. "It sounds like it's time for adjectives and adverbs."

WHAT ADJECTIVES ARE

We've already touched on the subject of adjectives. We talked about the articles *a, an,* or *the*, and we looked at possessive pronouns like *my, your, our, her, its,* and *their*. These words, if you remember, gave us some extra information about nouns. All **adjectives**, in fact, give extra information about nouns and pronouns—that's their job. Adjectives can give extra information in three ways: by describing, identifying, or quantifying.

DESCRIBING ADJECTIVES

A nice boy. A huge mess. A broken heart. Yikes! Adjectives give us extra information about a noun—maybe *too* much information—by describing it. Adjectives that describe—in other words, **describing adjectives**—are the most common kind, and you see them all the time. Describing adjectives answer the question "What kind?"

The *foolish* friend knew her crush was a *terrible* secret.

What kind of friend? A foolish friend. What kind of secret? A (gulp) terrible one. Adjectives are pretty useful, aren't they?

Adjectives usually come before the noun they modify, but they can also rename the subject of a sentence or appear after a linking verb connecting them to their noun. Look at this:

Charlie is *adorable.* Rosita is *lucky*.

When adjectives rename the subject of a sentence, like these do, they, too, answer the question "What kind?"

Here is a more typical describing adjective, next to its noun:

I wish I hadn't been on the date with Theo, the *boring* guy.

Notice how *boring*, which answers the question "What kind of guy?", is a participle form of the verb *bore*. Lots of verbs can be converted into adjectives by adding *-ing*, *-ed*, or *-en*. Here are some others: *exciting*, *respected*, *given* (like "a given name"). Neat, huh?

IDENTIFYING ADJECTIVES

Adjectives can also help you identify exactly what you're talking about. Let's say, just for fun, I'm in a room full of guys from Charlie's football team. Sure, they're all cute . . . but Charlie is the cutest, by far. If I want to point him out to someone, I have to be specific. I have to answer the question "Which one?"

That guy is adorable.
Those guys are Charlie's friends.

That and *those* are **identifying adjectives.** If you were paying attention while I blathered about pronouns (which I'm *sure* you were!), you've figured out by now that identifying adjectives are actually our old pals demonstrative pronouns: *this, that, these,* and *those*.

QUANTIFYING ADJECTIVES

Do you want to answer the burning question, "How many?" Then you have to use still more adjectives:

I saw *several* guys from school at the restaurant.
I saw *three* guys from school at the restaurant.

Yep, *several* and *three* are both adjectives! *Several*, *few*, *many*, and regular old numbers all answer the question "How many?" We call them **quantifying adjectives** since they show, as you've noticed, quantity.

PROPER ADJECTIVES

When an adjective is formed from a proper noun, like *American* or *Buddhist*, you have to capitalize the adjective the same way you capitalize the proper noun it's taken from.

ADJECTIVE CLAUSES

Some sentences have little groups of words wedged inside of them that give extra information about a subject. Look at this:

My house, *which is like a second home for Rosita*, sits right down the block from Rosita's house.

You see the subject, *my house*, and the verb, *sits*, but they're separated by a group of words: *which is like a second home for Rosita*. These words give us extra information about my house. Without them, you'd know where the house is, but you wouldn't know that it's important to Rosita. This whole group of words describes my house—so it's considered an adjective. In fact, we call it an **adjective clause**.

An adjective clause always begins with a relative pronoun: *who*, *whom*, *whose*, *which*, or *that*. In the example above, that little word *which* makes the whole group of words following it act like one giant adjective to describe *house*.

Adjective clauses often have commas around them, making them easy to spot.

There's one more thing you should know about identifying adjective clauses. Look again at our example:

My house, *which is like a second home for Rosita*, sits right down the block from Rosita's house.

The main verb in the sentence is *sits*—that's what my house is doing. But look inside the adjective clause—there's another verb right in there, *is*. Adjective clauses often contain a verb. Here are some more examples:

The house *sitting down the block* from Rosita's is mine.
The house *located up the block from mine* belongs to Rosita.

In these sentences, *sitting* and *located* are verbs, but they aren't the main verbs in the sentences. The main verbs are *is* and *belongs*. Notice that there is no subject that goes along those non-main verbs. Whenever you see a clause starting with *who*, *whom*, *whose*, *which*, or *that* that's followed by a verb and no subject, you know you're looking at an adjective clause.

RESTRICTED TERRITORY

Sometimes, adjective clauses are absolutely necessary–if you removed them, the sentence would mean something entirely different. Other times, you could leave them out without doing any harm to the sentence's meaning.

Here's an example of an adjective clause hard at work:

Hot guys *who love grammar* are hard to find.

We obviously have an adjective clause–there's a relative pronoun, *who*, followed by a verb but no subject. The adjective clause *who love grammar* describes *hot guys*. We definitely can't take that adjective clause out, because look what happens if we do:

Hot guys are hard to find.

Granted, the Charlie variety of hotness is a rare and beautiful thing. But there are plenty of other hot guys out there–I just don't notice them! We have to add the detail about loving grammar for my sentence to keep my intended meaning. Grammar-loving cuties are *definitely* a rare breed.

Let's look at an adjective clause that isn't quite so important:

Charlie, *who loves grammar*, is definitely a hot guy.

Just in case you didn't know enough about Charlie, I added a little more about him: I made the adjective clause *who loves grammar* modify Charlie. There's a big difference, though, between this example and the last one. In this sentence, if I leave out the adjective clause, the sentence would still be fine:

Charlie is definitely a hot guy.

I wanted to tell you that Charlie's hot–and whether the extra info is there or not, my message gets through loud and clear.

THE COMMA CONNECTION

Fine, you're saying, but so what? Well, look again at the two examples:

Hot guys *who love grammar* are hard to find.
Charlie, *who loves grammar*, is definitely a hot guy.

In the second sentence, I put commas around my adjective clause, but in the first sentence I didn't use any commas at all. The commas, small as they are, are really important—they tell you whether or not the adjective clause is absolutely necessary or whether you could safely take it out.

If you don't see any commas, the adjective clause limits—or restricts—the meaning of the noun it modifies. In other words, it's a **restrictive clause**. If you do see commas, the adjective clause doesn't limit—or doesn't restrict—the meaning. This kind of clause is **nonrestrictive**. Restrictive clauses narrow the meaning of the nouns they modify. Nonrestrictive ones just add more information.

In the first example, loving grammar is an essential part of the deal. I'm not talking about all hot guys, only those who love grammar. See? I've restricted the subject of my sentence, hot guys, to a smaller group of guys, hot guys who love grammar. I want that restricted meaning, so I leave the commas out. If I'd put them in and written *Hot guys, who love grammar, are hard to find*, it would sound as if I thought all hot guys love grammar. We know *that* isn't true. Hot guys who love grammar make a very small group indeed!

In the second sentence, you could take out the luscious fact that Charlie loves grammar and he'd still be hot. Definitely. The sentence is about his hotness. The adjective clause is nonrestrictive, more like an interruption to add something interesting—*very* interesting. No matter how interesting, though, it gets commas around it to point out that it's not essential to understanding the subject of the sentence.

TAKE IT OUT, TAKE IT ALL THE WAY OUT

If you can take the adjective clause out of the sentence without changing the sentence's meaning, the clause is nonrestrictive. Use commas around it.

APPOSITIVES

Sometimes, extra descriptions that aren't adjective clauses might pop up in commas to rename or describe a subject. Look at these examples:

My tiny planet, *the proverbial small world*, has only one Charlie in it.
My world, *unbelievably small*, has only one Charlie in it.

The proverbial small world is just another way of saying *my tiny planet*, and *unbelievably small* is an extra description of *my world*. Phrases like these, that rename or describe the subject of the sentence, are called **appositives**. Appositives are always set off with commas.

WHAT ADVERBS ARE

As we've seen, adjectives give extra information about nouns. But nouns aren't the only words that sometimes call for extra info. When it comes to modifying other parts of speech, call in the adverbs. **Adverbs** answer the question "How?" and they can modify verbs, adjectives, other adverbs, or even entire phrases.

ADVERBS MODIFYING VERBS

Here's some love advice from my sister, Marie:

A broken heart heals quickly.

That's great advice, but guess what's even more exciting: Both an adjective and an adverb make a guest appearance in that sentence! Remember that some adjectives answer the question "What kind?" and adverbs answer the question "How?" Well, let's find the adjective and adverb here: What kind of heart? Broken. How does it heal? Quickly.

Here's a sentence that shows another adverb in action, modifying a verb:

Rosita speaks *loudly* when she's excited.

How does Rosita speak? Loudly.

ADVERBS MODIFYING ADJECTIVES

Say you've got an adjective that's busy describing a noun, but you also want to describe the adjective. Adverbs can do the job:

Rosita had a *really* great time on her date with Charlie.

What kind of time? A great time. How great? Really great.

ADVERBS MODIFYING OTHER ADVERBS

It sounds like a cat chasing its tail, but sometimes you do need an adverb to modify *another* adverb. Actually, you probably use adverbs this way all the time without realizing it. Here's a common example:

Rosita tuned me out *very rudely* after I started talking.

Rudely is an adverb, and so is *very*. How did Rosita tune me out? Rudely. How rudely? Very rudely.

ADVERBS MODIFYING A PHRASE

When one word describes an entire phrase, that word is an adverb.

Getting over my crush on Charlie *quickly* can only make my life easier.

Getting over my crush on Charlie is the subject of the sentence. The verb *get*, in its handy present participle (*-ing*) form, together with the other words, acts as a noun. Since it's a whole phrase with a verb in it, you use the adverb *quickly*, not the adjective *quick*, to modify it.

Here's an example of the same adverb modifying a whole clause:

Whoever gets over her crushes *quickly* gets on with her life more easily.

By the way, I used the pronoun *her* in the clause *whoever gets over her crushes* because, even though *whoever* is indefinite, we've been talking about the crushes Rosita and I have. However, we can't really tell which gender *whoever* is from the context of the sentence. If you saw that sentence on a random quiz, you'd have to use *his* or *her*.

GOOD VS. EVIL

I got your attention, right? Okay, I confess, this section isn't really about any great battle over the fate of the world. But if you're worried about the fate of your grammar know-how, you'll still pay close attention.

Lots of people get confused over when to use *good* and *bad* versus *well* and *badly*. The trick is to remember that *good* and *bad* are *adjectives*, answering the question "What kind?" whereas *well* and *badly* are *adverbs*, answering the question "How?" If you want readers to know *how* Paramus did at the football game the other night, you wouldn't write:

WRONG: The Paramus High football team played bad.

Instead, you'd use an adverb:

RIGHT: The Paramus High football team played *badly*.

On the other hand, if you want to express *what kind* of team Paramus is, you use the adjective:

The Paramus High football team is bad.

Bad here renames the subject–it is an adjective connected to its noun by the linking verb *is*.

COMPARATIVES AND SUPERLATIVES

Certain types of adjectives and adverbs don't just describe one thing, but actually compare different things. **Comparative** adjectives and adverbs make a direct comparison between two things; **superlatives** compare three or more things.

COMPARATIVE

- Which would be *worse*: having to watch Rosita go out with my crush, or losing Rosita as a best friend?
- Rosita is a *better* friend to me than my old friend Lena was.

SUPERLATIVE

- The *worst* thing that could happen to me would be losing Rosita's friendship.
- Rosita is the *best* friend I've ever had.

To make some adjectives or adverbs comparative, add *-er*, changing *y*'s to *i*'s if need be. For others, you add the word *more* or the word *less*. Check your dictionary if you're not sure. To make adjectives or adverbs superlative, add *-est*, or add the word *most* or the word *least*:

The *sooner* I get over Charlie, the *less awful* I will feel.
I'm *least likely* to bail on Rosita.

ONE IS ENOUGH

Comparatives and superlatives do a great job of making a point. In fact, they do such a great job that you don't need to use more than one—and you shouldn't! Here's something Rosita does all the time that drives me crazy:

Mr. Millburn is the *most nastiest* teacher on the planet.

If he's the nastiest out of every single teacher (which is kind of harsh, but whatever), then he doesn't need to be the *most* nastiest, now does he?

TOO MUCH OF A GOOD THING

Adjectives and adverbs are great, fabulous, stupendous things and all, but it's pretty easy to overuse them. Read over your writing and see if any of the adjectives and adverbs you used are unnecessary. Sometimes a sentence can look a lot sleeker if you trim down these extra words and instead use more descriptive nouns or verbs. Check it out:

INSTEAD OF: Look at that tall building!
TRY: Look at that skyscraper!
INSTEAD OF: "Stop right there!" she said loudly.
TRY: "Stop right there!" she screamed.

YOUR TURN

In the following four sentences, underline each adjective, including articles and possessive pronouns, as well as describing, identifying, and quantifying adjectives. Extra credit! Find and label the comparatives and superlatives.

1. **Rosita, who is brilliant at post-date analysis, knows that I like thick, curly, dark hair, but Theo is only one among many guys with a head of terrific hair.**

2. **Charlie has that kind of hair, too.**

3. **When several guys have fabulous hair, I am going to go for the one who is smartest, funniest, and most interesting *under* his hair.**

4. **Which of those two guys fits that bill better?**

In the following four sentences, underline the adjectives and adverbs. Then indicate the word or group of words being modified by each adjective and adverb. If the adjective or adverb is misused, correct the mistake.

5. **I have got to stop thinking so often about Charlie, his great hair, and his smart, funny, interesting personality.**

6. **Obsession is not good, and I've got it bad.**

7. **An innocent bystander might even say my case of misplaced obsession is extreme, and Rosita's obliviousness makes it more worse.**

8. **Shake your head sadly, and get your most deepest sympathy out, too, because my obsession is going nowhere fast.**

In the following two sentences, fill in the blanks with a comparative or superlative form of the adjective/adverb supplied.

9. Crushes are ______ (*bad*) than bad hair days, but, let's face it, ______ (*horrible*) than cancer.

10. When it comes to my ______ (*bad*) nightmare, losing Rosita's friendship, the ______ (*simple*) solution of all would be to forget Charlie as soon as possible.

* * * * *

After Rosita left, I thought about all the stuff we'd just been talking about and all the questions that had run through my brain. It was a no-brainer which was more important to me, Rosita's friendship or my crush on Charlie. Charlie was great, fabulous, and all the other adjectives Rosita had tossed around. But Rosita was my best friend. Best friends don't come along every day, and they're worth more than almost anything else.

So how was I going to get over Charlie once and for all?

7

CHAPTER 7
OTHER PARTS OF SPEECH

"Pass me the Chunky Monkey."

I handed my older sister, Marie, the nearly empty Ben & Jerry's pint, then took the one in front of her, New York Super Fudge Chunk, and spooned out the last few bites.

"Are we seriously pathetic, or what?" Marie asked.

"I guess this is pretty clichéd," I admitted, "two girls eating ice cream to take their minds off guys."

"You know, some clichés exist for a reason," Marie said. "Ice cream—the good stuff, not that lame junk, frozen yogurt—really does help, doesn't it?"

"I guess." I paused, plopping my spoon down on the kitchen table. "Do you feel any better?"

She shrugged. "Not really, but it sure did taste good."

I cracked a smile. The truth was, Marie required ice cream far more than I did. I was still mooning over Charlie, who was out with Rosita at that very moment bowling at some new place called Spooky Lanes, and I'd filled my sister in on that situation. But Marie had been dumped the day before by her boyfriend, Ben. They'd been dating for almost two months, and then suddenly he said it was over. Today she'd found out it was because he'd moved on to another girl.

"Sara Owens," Marie said, shaking her head. "Why Sara? I mean, I never thought she was all that special."

"She's nothing next to you," I said. "She's a total ditz." I didn't really know Sara, but I was perfectly willing to hate her out of sisterly duty. "Listen, I know you really liked Ben, but if he could leave you for Sara, doesn't that tell you something about him?"

"I guess. Yeah, I know, you're right. I just wish I could stop thinking about the jerk."

"At least you know he's a jerk," I said. "Charlie's, like, Mr. Amazing, but he's also Mr. Rosita to me."

"You know what our problem is?"

"We're out of ice cream?"

"No, seriously, what we need is confidence. That's what Sara has, I think. She's so sure of herself that it does a mental trick on guys like Ben, convincing them she's worth it. And the same thing goes for Rosita. You know I love her, but the reason she's always got a date on Saturday night is that she never worries she *won't*."

It was true, I knew. But somehow I didn't think Rosita could teach me confidence as easily as I was imparting my grammar wisdom to her.

Marie looked down at our empty pints of ice cream. "I feel gross," she said.

"Me too."

We were quiet for a minute, and then she met my gaze across the table. "Are you thinking what I'm thinking?"

"I don't know. . . ."

"Leftover mac-and-cheese!"

We got up and headed over to the fridge. Sometimes, ice cream by itself just isn't enough.

THE LEFTOVER PARTS OF SPEECH

You may not have known all the different rules about nouns, verbs, adjectives, and adverbs, but I bet you knew those names. See, they're the flashier parts of speech, the ones that get all the attention. But there are other parts of speech that work behind the scenes, doing their jobs without making a big fuss. Don't ask me why these leftover parts of speech don't get to share in the glory: They're the ones that hold whole groups of words together.

THE PREPOSITION

Adjectives, as we've seen, answer the questions "What kind?" "Which one?" and "How many?" And adverbs answer the question "How?" That's all well and good. But there are other questions that pop up as well, like "Where?," "When?," and "How so?" And it's up to another part of speech to answer these.

Who is this superhero of grammar? We call it the **preposition**. There are lots of different prepositions, as you'll see in a minute. Prepositions introduce prepositional phrases, which contain nouns and, sometimes, adjectives. A **prepositional phrase**, like an adjective or an adverb, modifies another word in a sentence, usually a noun or a verb.

WHERE?

One kind of preposition tells you about location—where one noun is in relation to another. Some common prepositions of this type are *above*, *across*, *below*, *by*, *between*, *in*, *at*, *over*, *under*, and *to*. Here are two examples:

The ice cream is *inside the freezer*. (At least, it was until Marie and I got *to it*!)

You can also string together more than one prepositional phrase, if you like:

The ice cream is *inside the freezer by the ice cube tray*. (At least, it was until Marie and I got *to it*!)

A prepositional phrase needs a noun or noun substitute. In the above examples, the nouns are *freezer* and *ice cube tray*. These are called **objects** of a preposition; without them, a preposition is pretty useless. If I told you that the ice cream was just "inside," you'd have no idea what I meant. Inside what? The complete prepositional phrase always includes the rest of the info—*inside the freezer*.

Note: Prepositional phrases do not contain verbs. If you see a verb, it's not a prepositional phrase. Remember, though, that some verbs can act like nouns!

WHEN?

Prepositions can also express time relationships. Some common examples are *after*, *before*, *by* (in its other sense of "before this time"), *during*, *until*, *since*, and *at*, when followed by a time noun. Here are some sample sentences:

You never realize how much you're eating *during a pig-out session.*
Marie and I have been pigging out *since three.*

Some prepositions, like *after* and *since*, can also act like other parts of speech. Don't panic. Just check whether there's a verb in the phrase. If there's no verb, you've got a prepositional phrase. Take this sentence for example:

Marie and I have been pigging out *since we arrived home* at three.

Here the word *since* is followed not only by the noun *we* but the verb *arrived*. In fact, *we arrived home* is a whole sentence, with subject, verb and object, and so *since* is definitely not being used as a preposition. (It's a subordinating conjunction, if you really must know, and we're covering those next!)

PREPOSITIONAL PRONOUNS

Remember subjective and objective case from our chapter on pronouns? The subjective case is *I*, *we*, *you*, *he*, *she*, *it*, and *they*; the objective is *me*, *us*, *you*, *him*, *her*, *it*, and *them*. A prepositional phrase will always use pronouns in their *objective* case. In the sentence above, you could also tell that *since* is not a preposition by looking at the pronoun following it. *We* cannot be the object of the prepositional phrase because it's in the subjective case. Try impressing people with *that* nugget of knowledge at parties!

HOW SO?

There's a catchall category for those prepositions that describe a relationship unrelated to space or time. A few examples of these words are *as*, *except*, *of*, *regarding*, *for*, *like*, and *to* (in its sense of "from the perspective of": *It seems that way to me*).

Here's how they might look in a sentence:

For once I wish I could leave some ice cream in the carton!

All prepositional phrases modify another word in the sentence. That word is almost always a noun or a verb. We'll practice picking out those words at the end of this chapter, but here's a little pointer in the meantime. If the prepositional phrase comes at the beginning or end of a sentence, as in our example above, it's probably modifying a verb—in this case, *wish*.

LIKE, IT'S A PREPOSITION

If you want to be *like everyone else*, misuse the word *like*. *Like* is a preposition, except when you use it as a verb (as in, for instance, *I like Charlie*). Look at these common misuses:

WRONG: I make this mistake, *like*, all the time—but never in an email to grammar-god Charlie.

Don't use *like* as an interjection.

WRONG: It's not *like* Charlie is a perfect human being. But he'd notice that kind of mistake.

Don't use *like* as a subordinating conjunction and follow it with a subject (*he*) and verb (*is*). Use *as if* or *as though* in those situations instead:

RIGHT: It's not *as if* Charlie is a perfect human being.

ACCESSORIZE, ACCESSORIZE

Okay, let's review. If a sentence were an outfit, your basic T-shirt and jeans would be the subject and predicate. But you can see how other words can get involved—sometimes singly, and sometimes in small clauses or phrases—to help clothe the sentence. Adjectives, for example, dress up nouns, and phrases that might be composed of lots of words can accessorize a sentence, making it even more descriptive.

So let's accessorize:

At the football game, Rosita met an incredible guy.

Here the first four words work together as a prepositional phrase. But wait! Now there are three nouns in the sentence: *game*, *Rosita*, and *guy*. How are we supposed to tell which one is the subject?

WORK BACKWARD

The secret way of finding the subject is to look for the main verb, the one that tells you what happens, and then figure out who or what did that action. In this case the main verb is *met*, Rosita is definitely the one doing the meeting, and the incredible guy is the one being met. A person or thing being acted on by a verb is called a **direct object** and is part of the predicate. Just as a football game has a quarterback, a play (or action) and a receiver, so does this sentence: *Rosita* is the quarterback, *met* is the pass, and *an incredible guy* is the receiver.

THE CONJUNCTION

As you already know, sometimes you need to join together two or more nouns, verbs, adjectives, adverbs, or even whole groups of words. There are a couple of ways to do this.

COORDINATING CONJUNCTIONS

Check out these two beautiful sentences:

Ice cream and veggie stir-fry don't make a bad combination.
The ice cream seemed to fly *out of the bowl and into my mouth.*

In the first sentence, the two subjects, *ice cream* and *veggie stir-fry*, are joined by *and*. In the second sentence, the two prepositional phrases *out of the bowl* and *into my mouth* are also joined by *and*. *And* is one example of a **coordinating conjunction**—a small word that joins single words and other small units of grammar.

Nope, sorry, being able to coordinate your clothes so that everything matches won't help you here! This is a different kind of coordinating. A coordinating conjunction is always used between *parts of sentences that are equal*. In other words, it goes between two adverbs, or two noun phrases, or two whole sentences, or . . . well, you get the picture! You just have to make sure that the two things being joined by the conjunction match each other as units of grammar. (Hey, it kind of *is* like coordinating clothes!) Here is a full list of coordinating conjunctions: *and*, *but*, *or*, *nor*, *for*, *so*, and *yet*.

How did *for* get on that list? Isn't *for* a preposition? Yes, it is, if it's followed by a noun and no verb. Sometimes, though, we use *for* in its sense of "because," for English is a crazy, unruly language:

We ate *for* hours, *for* we were bummed.

In the first use, *for* is followed by a noun, *hours*, and only that noun, so it must be a preposition. In the second use, *for* is a conjunction because a pronoun and a verb follow it (*we* and *were*). Remember also that *we* is in the subjective case, and so it can't be the object of a prepositional phrase.

WHAT'S THE POINT?

A coordinating conjunction can show the similarities between words or phrases, or it can show the differences between them, depending on which one you use. Check it out:

Marie *and* I were feeling bummed.

The conjunction in that sentence shows the similarity between my sister and me.

Marie and I were feeling bummed, *but* Rosita was in heaven.

In that sentence, *but* points out how different we are from Rosita.

Notice also that in the first example, *and* coordinates two matching parts of speech: Even though *Marie* is a noun and *I* is a pronoun, both are of equal rank as units of grammar. In the second example, *but* coordinates two whole clauses, complete with subjects and verbs.

Joining together two whole sentences is one of the coolest things conjunctions can do. In fact, if you've got a sentence, the *only* way to connect it to another sentence is with a conjunction. Two whole sentences joined together by a coordinating conjunction result in a **compound sentence**. Why would you want such a thing? Trust me, you do, because using conjunctions on this scale helps you express your reasoning. Conjunctions between clauses tell your reader how your thoughts fit together.

CORRELATIVE CONJUNCTIONS

Coordinating conjunctions are like little Lone Rangers, joining things together on their own. Some conjunctions aren't so independent, and they rely on a partner to help them. Here are some common pairs that travel together: *both . . . and*; *either . . . or*; *neither . . . nor*; *not only . . . but also*; and *whether . . . or*.

How do you put one of these pairs to use? Here we go:

Both Marie *and* I were feeling really bummed.
Neither Marie *nor* I could stop eating.

These pairs are loyal, so you have to keep them together—never mix and match. (Hey, your fashion know-how comes in handy again!) These partner-in-crime conjunctions are called **correlative conjunctions**.

Here's a heads up on another common grammar problem. Don't get bamboozled by the correlative into forgetting that a pronoun has to take the subjective case if it's together in a phrase with a verb:

WRONG: Neither Marie *nor me* could get full.
RIGHT: *Neither* Marie *nor I* could get full.

SUBORDINATING CONJUNCTIONS

Here's an important fact: Conjunctions go way beyond the basic coordinating conjunctions *if*, *and*, and *but* to include *because*, *since*, *although*, *so*, *yet*, *that*, *unless*, and *while*, just to mention a few. Think about these words, and how lost you'd be without them. There's almost no way to explain the logic of your statements without conjunctions.

Let's take a look at an example:

We ate everything in the fridge *because* we were feeling really bummed.

Here, the conjunction *because* joins together two ideas. One of those ideas, however, is more important. The main idea in the sentence is that we ate everything in the fridge. Why did we do it? We were bummed. Those new conjunctions I just mentioned—*because*, *since*, *although*, *so*, *yet*, *that*, *unless*, and *while*—introduce ideas that are less important than a main idea in a sentence.

Because these conjunctions introduce less important ideas, we call them **subordinating conjunctions**. Your boss might call you and your coworkers "subordinates" because you're less important than she is, and you have to work for her. When a clause is subordinate, it works for the benefit of another clause.

When you use a subordinating conjunction, the result is called a **complex**

sentence instead of a compound sentence. If you use *both* subordinating conjunctions and coordinating conjunctions to join three or more clauses, you've got yourself a **compound-complex sentence**:

Because we were feeling really bummed, we ate everything in the fridge, and still neither Marie nor I could get full.

By the way, a subordinating conjunction can be more than one word long, as you'll see in some of these examples: *after*, *because*, *before*, *except that*, *even if*, *as if*, *unless*, *while*, *until*, *since*, *that*, *so*, and *in case*:

Even though we ate everything in the fridge, neither Marie nor I could get full.

Some subordinating conjunctions you've met before, as other parts of speech. *For*, *before*, *since*, and *until* can be prepositions, for example. *That* can be a demonstrative pronoun or relative pronoun. In fact, three other relative pronouns, *who*, *whom*, and *which*, often introduce subordinate clauses too. As always, the key is to look for a verb. You can recognize when a word is being used as a subordinating conjunction because it will be followed by a whole clause, including subject and verb, with the verb in agreement with the subject. Here are two examples using *after*, first as a preposition, then as a subordinating conjunction:

I will probably regret pigging out *after all*.
I will probably regret pigging out *after I wake up in the morning*.

In the first sentence, only a noun follows *after*. But in the second sentence, *after* is followed by a whole group of words. *I wake up in the morning* has a subject, *I*, contains the verb *wake*, and expresses a complete thought. The subordinating conjunction *after* takes that complete thought and puts it in the service of what's called the main clause, *I will probably regret all this pigging out*. By using *after* to join the two clauses, you learn the answer to the question "When?" When is this regret going to surface? Now you know: not until tomorrow, mercifully.

WHERE SUBORDINATE CLAUSES GO

Notice how in our earlier example, the conjunction *even though* started its sample sentence so that the subordinate clause came first, but in the sentence right above, the subordinate clause beginning with *after* comes at the end. You can also put subordinate clauses into the middle of sentences, like this:

The pigging out *that Marie and I do tonight*
will catch up with us tomorrow.

TO COMMA OR NOT?

Like adjective clauses, subordinate clauses can be restrictive or nonrestrictive. Use a pair of commas for nonrestrictive ones, just as you do for nonrestrictive adjective clauses:

In general, pigging out, *which Marie and I are doing tonight*,
is a bad strategy.

THE INTERJECTION

Hey! Ready for a super-easy part of speech? Sometimes little words or phrases, like *yikes*, *ouch*, *hey*, *wow*, and *eek*, burst their way into or between sentences. They express surprise or some other kind of emotion, and they're called **interjections**.

Interjections usually show a pretty strong emotion, so when they're used all by themselves they're often followed by exclamation points:

Did we really eat all that? Eek!

When interjections don't need to be this intense, you can stick them inside a sentence. Just use a comma to give it a little breathing room from the rest of the sentence, like this:

Yikes, that was a lot of food.

YOUR TURN

In the following five sentences, underline each of the prepositional phrases and indicate the word it modifies. Remember, prepositional phrases can act like adjectives or adverbs. Remember, too, that if a verb is part of the phrase, it's not a prepositional phrase, unless the verb is acting like a noun.

1. I hope Rosita will stop asking for my help on her emails after this date, for I am getting tired of writing them.

2. On the other hand, I can't wait for my Toasters CD from her.

3. Through their catchy tunes, that group of musicians makes me feel like dancing and singing.

4. After all that ice cream, I'll need to dance all night, just to return to my normal size.

5. To Ben & Jerry's, Marie and I have got to be the ideal customer, with our dedication to finishing whole cartons of the stuff.

In the following five sentences, label each coordinating conjunction (CC), correlative conjunction (CR), or subordinating conjunction (SC). Put brackets around subordinate clauses. Extra credit! Identify the prepositions (PP), relative pronouns (RP), and demonstrative pronouns (DP).

6. Marie thought that we should stop after the mac-and-cheese, but I decided that we needed to finish with something healthy, since we were feeling guilty.

7. Either Marie or I should have made the fridge off limits after the mac-and-cheese.

8. Instead, we kept eating those kinds of food until midnight came and went.

9. After midnight, Marie and I pigged out in our pj's, which were more comfortable than our jeans had been.

10. Marie, whom I usually admire for her healthy eating habits, taught me a thing or two about junk food and being bummed.

* * * * *

By the time Rosita called later that night to fill me in on how incredibly and amazingly fantastic her date had been, Marie and I had topped off our macaroni-and-cheese with some stir-fried veggies (to balance out all those empty calories), and I didn't think I'd be eating ever again.

"You know what the best part about tonight was?" Rosita said before she hung up.

"Hmm?"

"Well, at first I was kind of nervous, deep down, that maybe you were the one he really liked, since he loved those emails you wrote so much. But tonight it was just us, and we had a great time. We really do have a lot in common, even though I'm not a grammar whiz like you guys."

"That's great." It was, right? I had proof now, just like Rosita, that the tiny little suspicion we'd both been secretly harboring was wrong.

It was a really weird feeling, relief and disappointment all jumbled up into one.

CHAPTER 8
PUNCTUATION, PART I

After Rosita's blissed-out phone call, I was pretty sure that my grammatical services wouldn't be needed anymore. Unfortunately, the following Friday afternoon I learned I was wrong.

"I wish I knew for sure what Charlie wanted," Rosita said with a dramatic sigh as she settled into her usual spot on my bed.

"Um, I think we're clear on that," I said. "You."

"Yeah, I know he likes me, but does he want this to be a relationship? Or just a casual thing?"

"What do *you* want?"

"I don't know. Normally I like to keep my options open, but with Charlie, I think I'm ready to have a boyfriend. I don't want to scare him, though. See, he sent me an email about 'hanging out this weekend,' and he mentioned a homecoming dance at River Dell, but he didn't actually come out and ask whether I wanted to go with him. Homecoming dances are totally couple things, right?"

"Sometimes, I guess." What was she doing asking me? I'd certainly never been part of a couple before.

"So I need to write back, and you need to help me."

I groaned. "I thought you were over needing help."

"Yeah, but this is different. I'm afraid those bat emoticons might mean he's scared to commit—you know, like a subliminal signal? I need to make sure that whatever I say to him now comes out just right, so there's no confusion. You know I'm rotten at this stuff. What if I accidentally write something wrong and it has a totally different meaning?"

"Okay, you're right, this *is* important," I said. "It's that whole defining-a-relationship stage." Didn't I sound like an expert? That's what a subscription to *YM* and an older sister will get you. "Let's do it."

I switched on the computer. "If you're worried about saying something he could misinterpret, you're going to have to work on good old punctuation."

WHAT PUNCTUATION IS

When it comes to **punctuation marks**, your main options are the period, question mark, exclamation point, comma, semicolon, colon, apostrophe, and quotation mark. Punctuation holds sentences together, as you know from our first chapter, but it also keeps the right *parts* of sentences separated. We touched on this idea earlier, when we looked at restrictive and nonrestrictive adjective clauses. Sometimes the words in a sentence can have a totally different meaning if the wrong punctuation mark is used, or the right one in the wrong place, or the wrong one in the right place, or—I think you get the picture!

COMMAS

You've already met some kinds of punctuation that go at the ends of sentences. Commas work on the inside, and they help turn sentences from long strings of words into ideas that make clear sense.

Commas are a lot like your favorite pair of jeans. They sometimes even come in pairs. Like jeans, the comma has a ton of different uses, and when it fits right, it makes all the difference. If you're anything like me, when you shop for jeans you take your time finding the perfect pair. (I'm a fan of low-rise boot-cut, if you care.) So why not take some time to master the comma, and you'll be one step closer to some fine-looking sentences! Here's the lowdown on how you'll want to use it.

COMPOUND SENTENCES

When you form a **compound sentence** (two main clauses with a coordinating conjunction), it's a good idea to stick in a comma before the conjunction:

Rosita thinks she needs my help, but I think it's time for me to butt out of things between her and Charlie.

INTERRUPTIONS

Sometimes a word or group of words in a sentence sounds dropped in, almost as if it were interrupting to say, "Oh, by the way. . . ." Chances are, it's a **nonrestrictive element**. Regardless of the length of the interruption, when you're setting off a nonrestrictive element, you use a pair of commas. This sentence, for example, illustrates my point. (Ha!) Remember, a nonrestrictive element is one that you can take out of the sentence without changing its meaning. Here's an example of each:

RESTRICTIVE: Students *caught cheating on exams* should automatically fail the class.

The participial phrase *caught cheating on exams* limits who automatically fails: not *all* students, only those caught cheating. It's restrictive, since without it the sentence takes on a whole different meaning. Restrictive phrases don't get commas.

NONRESTRICTIVE: Students, *chewing gum and listening to headphones*, sat in the principal's office.

This time the participial phrases *chewing gum* and *listening to headphones* aren't necessary to the purpose of the sentence, which is to tell us where the students are. They're nonrestrictive phrases, so they call for commas. And since they're compounded, you only need one pair of commas to go around both of them.

SINGLES NIGHT FOR COMMAS

Skip the pair if the nonrestrictive element comes at the beginning or end of the sentence. You only need one comma then.

INTRODUCTIONS

When a sentence has an introduction to the main idea, you use a comma to put a pause between the introduction and the rest of the sentence. An introduction can sometimes be just one word, and sometimes it can be a whole phrase. Look at these:

Finally, I can stop writing Rosita's emails.

Since she started learning grammar, Rosita has become a more confident writer.

> **DON'T RUSH IT**
>
> Remember that the comma doesn't go in until after the introduction part of the sentence is over, no matter how long the introduction seems to last.

CONTRASTING ELEMENTS

Sometimes you need to emphasize what you're saying by pointing out what you're *not* saying. In other words, you have to *contrast* what you're saying. When you toss a contrasting element into a sentence, you stick it between commas to set it apart. Check out this example:

It's Rosita, *not me*, whom Charlie likes.

It's really, really important that you understand, without any confusion, exactly whom Charlie likes! It's Rosita. *Not me!*

INTERJECTIONS

Remember when I talked about these little zingers? When they introduce, end, or even interrupt sentences, they need commas, like this:

I thought I was over Charlie a long time ago, but, *yikes*, I learned fast how wrong I was.

DIRECT ADDRESS

When you're talking to someone and you call out to them, you use commas around the word you're using to address the person, which could be their name or something more general like *sir*, *miss*, or *you*. Check it out:

Look, *you*, do you want to learn grammar or not?
Sir, please don't yell at me.

TAG QUESTIONS

A tag question is a question that likes to play tag. Okay, it's not really; wouldn't that be weird? Actually, a tag question is a little question that gets tacked onto the end of a regular sentence, using a single comma:

Tag questions are pretty simple, *aren't they?*

LISTS, DATES, AND ADDRESSES

Whenever you make a list, always check it twice and put commas between each of the items:

My dream meal would include *spinach pizza, onion rings, and cinnamon toast.*

THE FINAL *AND*

Some teachers don't want you to use a comma before the final *and*; others do. In general, if the items on your list are short, you can safely leave out the last comma if you really want to. But for items that are longer than a word or two, a comma before your final *and* makes your list a little clearer. Like this:

OKAY: My closet contains lots of shoes, a thousand shirts and a gazillion pairs of jeans.

BETTER: My closet contains lots of shoes, a thousand shirts, and a gazillion pairs of jeans.

If you're writing a date, you need a comma between the different units of time, including the year and the rest of the sentence, if the year isn't the end of the sentence. The only place you don't put a comma is between the month and day of the month:

On Saturday, December 20, 2003, I took my first SAT test.

If you're writing only the month and the year, you don't need a comma:

I took my first SAT test in December 2003.

You need tons of commas when you're writing an address, too. The only place where you don't need one is before the zip code. Here's how an address should look:

I live at 555 Main Street, Paramus, New Jersey 07652.

QUOTATIONS

When you quote someone else, you need a comma between the words explaining who's talking, called a **signal phrase**, and the quotation itself:

My mother always tells me, "One day you'll meet the right boy."

Sometimes you switch the order, putting the quotation before the signal phrase. You still need the comma, but you put it inside the quotation mark:

"One day you'll meet the right boy," my mother says.

The only time you don't use a comma is when the quotation ends with an exclamation point or a question mark, because that would just be punctuation overload:

"Will I ever meet a guy who's right for me?" I asked my mother.

WHEN TO LEAVE COMMAS OUT

It's starting to seem like commas are used for just about everything, right? Well, just be careful, because there are times when you *shouldn't* use a comma, and knowing when *not* to use a comma is just as important as knowing when to use one!

Here are some common dangerous comma situations you should watch out for.

NO COMMAS BETWEEN SUBJECTS AND VERBS, VERBS AND OBJECTS, AND PREPOSITIONS AND OBJECTS

Certain parts of speech need to be linked together without commas because they operate as a unit. Here are three example sentences of WRONG comma usage, followed by the correct sentence.

- Subject and verb:

WRONG: *Marie and I, ate* too much from the kitchen.

- Verb and object:

WRONG: Marie and I *ate, too much* from the kitchen.

- Preposition and object:

WRONG: Marie and I ate too much *from, the kitchen.*
RIGHT: Marie and I ate too much from the kitchen.

NO COMMAS IN SHORT LISTS

When you have a list with only two items on it, you should never put a comma in the way, even if the items are pretty long. For instance:

WRONG: Rosita, and Charlie seem to make a great couple.
RIGHT: Rosita and Charlie seem to make a great couple.
WRONG: After all that snacking the other night, I need to do extra time on the treadmill, and the stationary bike tomorrow.
RIGHT: After all that snacking the other night, I need to do extra time on the treadmill and the stationary bike tomorrow.

COMPOUND SENTENCES: THE BIG EXCEPTION

If you've got two complete thoughts joined by a coordinating conjunction—that is, a list of two sentences—you put a comma in:

After all that snacking the other night, I need to do extra time on the treadmill, and Marie needs to hit the stationary bike.

NO COMMAS BEFORE THE FIRST OR AFTER THE LAST ITEM IN A SERIES

Even though commas are used to separate items in a list of three or more, you *don't* use commas at the beginning or at the end of a list or series. Here are some examples:

WRONG: By the time you're finished this book you'll *be, relieved*, thrilled, and adored for your grammar.
RIGHT: By the time you're finished this book you'll *be relieved*, thrilled, and adored for your grammar.

THE SEMICOLON

Remember the story of Goldilocks, that little blonde girl who was always having problems with things being too big or too small, until she'd find something that was "just right?" Well, the semicolon is the answer to Goldilocks' dreams in the world of punctuation. It creates a pause in writing that's stronger than a comma, but not quite as strong as a period.

PINCH-HITTING FOR . . . THE PERIOD

Let's say you've got two sentences that are related. You want to show that they're related, and so a period between them seems too final. On the other hand, they have enough independence that you don't want to join them with a conjunction. Voila—a perfect time to use the semicolon. The semicolon fuses two clauses into one sentence without extra words, while still keeping a clear boundary between them. Here's how:

Rosita needs to realize she can write these emails on her own. She's a perfectly intelligent girl.

OR

Rosita needs to realize she can write these emails on her own, because she's a perfectly intelligent girl.

BECOMES

Rosita needs to realize she can write these emails on her own; she's a perfectly intelligent girl.

Just make sure you only use the semicolon when the two ideas really are connected, and if the connection is crucial, use a conjunction to nail it down for the reader.

WRONG: Rosita needs to realize she can write these emails on her own; I wish my computer would stop freezing.

Both sentences contain two clauses that could be their own sentences, so they've fulfilled that part of the semicolon requirements. However, there isn't a strong enough connection between the two ideas. Yeah, emails and computers are related, but the main action of my wishing that the computer would stop freezing doesn't add any extra information to the idea that Rosita needs to write her own emails.

> **IMAGINE THAT**
>
> A great trick to help out is to imagine the conjunction that would fit in the sentence if you took the semicolon out. In one variation of our sample sentence, I used the conjunction *because* to show that the second clause explains why Rosita should write the emails herself. If you can't think of a conjunction that would make sense, you shouldn't be using a semicolon.

TRANSITIONS

Another good time to use a semicolon is when you have two closely related ideas that *do* have a word joining them—a **transitional word** (or words) like *therefore, however, also, in fact, even so*, or *on the other hand*. These words are not conjunctions, although they do describe the logical links between two clauses. You might be tempted to use a comma, but, in fact, you *have* to use a semicolon if you want to join ideas related by transitional words. Otherwise, stick to the period. Check it out:

Rosita is convinced that she can't write a good email to Charlie by herself; therefore, she's making me write all of her emails for her.

PINCH-HITTING FOR . . . THE COMMA

You already know that you usually use commas to break up three or more items in a list, like this:

My dream meal would include spinach pizza,
onion rings, and cinnamon toast.

But when the items in a list already contain commas or other marks of punctuation, using a semicolon instead of a comma to separate them will make the sentence easier to read. Semicolons work so well in this situation that you should use them even when just one of the items has a comma inside of it:

My favorite books include *Wuthering Heights*, by Emily Bronte; *A Tale of Two Cities* and *Great Expectations*, by Charles Dickens; and anything by L. M. Montgomery.

THE COLON

The colon is another one of those pieces of punctuation that gives you a "pause" while you're reading. But you only use it in special situations. A colon can be used to introduce an example or explanation, a series or list, or a long quotation. Colons can only come after a main clause, complete, as you know, with subject and verb.

INTRODUCTIONS

I've been using colons throughout this book to introduce examples, *like this*:

Hello, I am an example.

You can also use a colon to introduce an example that's all part of one sentence on the same line:

My favorite books are classics: *Wuthering Heights*, for example.

Colons can also introduce explanations. Check it out:

Here's how to win the guy of your dreams, according to Rosita: First, meet him at a football game, and then have your best friend write all of your emails for you.

Remember the lists and series I've talked about, and how you use either commas or semicolons to separate them, but never to introduce them? Well, sometimes you introduce a series with a colon, as long as it has a main clause to follow:

WRONG: My favorite foods are: spinach pizza, onion rings, and cinnamon toast.
RIGHT: Here are my favorite foods: spinach pizza, onion rings, and cinnamon toast.

You can *also* use a colon to introduce a quote, provided, once again, you precede it with an independent clause:

WRONG: My favorite line from *The Princess Bride* is when Wesley tells Buttercup: "As you wish."
RIGHT: Wesley says my favorite line from *The Princess Bride* to Buttercup: "As you wish."

One last introduction for you is when you're writing a business letter. Use a colon after the greeting line to introduce the rest:

Dear Ms. Martinez:
Congratulations–you've won a million dollars!

In a less formal letter or in an email, you can use a comma after the greeting.

SEPARATIONS

Colons also put some separation in when you need it for things like telling time, expressing a ratio (I know, math, ick!), or breaking up a title from a subtitle. Here are some examples:

TIME: 3:29 P.M.
RATIO: The girls always outnumber the guys at school dances by a ratio of about 2:1.
TITLE/SUBTITLE: The next book I write is going to be called *Out of the Middle: How to Stay out of Your Best Friend's Love Life.*

YOUR TURN

Punctuate the following sentences as needed.

1. Who knew that I would become the voice of Rosita

2. Not only am I writing her emails but yikes I'm actually asking Charlie to get serious with her

3. That kind of forwardness which I don't normally have would be really handy in certain situations telling off Sara explaining myself to my mother when I'm late and of course going after Charlie way back in seventh grade

4. When I think of all the time I've wasted being shy I blame me not anyone else because there's no one else to blame is there

5. I'll have to kiss all those opportunities I had goodbye the sweetheart dance on April 15 1999 the sock hop in November 2000 and the Fourth of July party at 35 Dayton Way Paramus New Jersey

6. What I should do now if I can relocate my sanity is take a nice long deep breath and say Arianna you've come a long way baby

7. You might be a little shy but you've got a great friend in Rosita I'll continue feeling better

8. Next I suppose I'll eat all the ice cream that I can find and finally my heartache will be gone

9. I'll let you know if any of this stuff works after I do it okay

10. Don't hold your breath though it seems like a long shot

* * * * *

Rosita and I finally managed to type up an email that got across her interest in the dance—and in something more serious with Charlie—without seeming too needy. We clicked SEND and then decided to call it quits for the afternoon.

I was so used to logging into Rosita's email that I almost slipped and typed in her password when I went to check my own inbox later that night. As a result, when I saw the email with the subject "dance?" I assumed I really had accidentally gone back to her account.

But when I opened the message, it was very clearly addressed to me. I scanned the perfectly written email quickly, my jaw dropping open. I couldn't believe this was actually happening!

9

CHAPTER 9
PUNCTUATION, PART II

I called Rosita as soon as I knew she'd be awake Saturday morning and immediately filled her in on my news. Someone had sent me an *anonymous* invitation to a homecoming dance the following weekend, from an email address I didn't recognize.

"Oh, my God! Do you have any idea who it is?" she asked.

I paused. For one terrible moment the night before, I'd wondered if it could be Charlie. But I knew he really liked Rosita, and he wasn't the kind of guy who'd ask out her best friend behind her back. I just couldn't think who else it would be.

"This is so cool," Rosita said. "You have a secret admirer! What's the email like?"

"It's kind of sweet. I mean, he says we don't know each other that well, but he'd *'love to get to know me better,'* because he thinks I have a great smile and *'a funny sense of humor.'* And Rosita, the whole thing is written *perfectly*, without a single grammar mistake!"

"Oh, my God," she repeated. "When's the wedding?"

I laughed. "Hey, did Charlie write back?"

"Yeah. He totally got my hint, just like you thought he would. He asked if I wanted to come to the dance with him, and he even said something about wanting his friends to meet his *girlfriend*."

"Rosi, that's so great!" I really meant it, too. I was a little sad that Charlie and I had never had our chance, but I could see how right he and Rosita were for each other. She'd never sounded anything but terrified to be called someone's girlfriend before.

It was more than time for me to move on, and I was okay with that. I just wondered if my secret email guy was really the right one for the job.

"I'm just going to take a quick shower, and then I'll come over," Rosita said. "I want to read every word of your email. We can brainstorm a list of possible guys who might have sent it, and then you'll do me one tiny favor."

"What's that?"

"Well, I have to write back to Charlie . . . and you said we still needed to finish punctuation, right?"

"Yeah, we do. Okay, fine, we'll do that today. See you soon."

THE APOSTROPHE

In my opinion, apostrophes don't get the respect they deserve. They're always getting stuck in the wrong spot, or even left out altogether. Okay, maybe I can relate to that feeling more than you can, but misused apostrophes are a special pet peeve of mine. See, messing up the apostrophe in a sentence may not seem like a big deal, but it can totally change the sentence's meaning. So let me set the record straight–right here, right now–about when and how to use these little guys.

OWNERSHIP

The first reason to use an apostrophe is when you want to show ownership–meaning, in regular English, to show that something belongs to something or someone else. For most singular nouns, you add an apostrophe and an *s* to show possession, like this:

I wasn't sure how confident I was in *Rosita's* plan to figure out the identity of my admirer.

Even when the noun ends in the letter *s*, you still usually follow this simple routine:

I wish my house came later on the school bus's route.

Sometimes, though, if it sounds better to leave off the extra *s*, you can do that, and just end the word with an apostrophe. Back in the section on semicolons, I wanted to make the word *Goldilocks* possessive, to modify *dreams*. *Goldilocks's dreams* was too awkward, so I wrote *Goldilocks' dreams* instead.

POSSESSIVE PLURAL NOUNS

When you need to make a plural noun possessive, it's pretty similar to what you do with singular nouns. You add an apostrophe and an *s*. But for plural nouns that end in the letter *s*, you add only an apostrophe:

The line for the *women's* bathroom is always longer than the line for the *men's* bathroom.

BUT

My *cats'* favorite spot to hide is under my bed.

NUMBER COMES BEFORE POSSESSION

The sentence about my cats is a purrfect example of why it's important to put the apostrophe in the right place. If you put it between the *t* and the *s*, it would look as if I had just one cat, when I really have two!

POSSESSIVE COMPOUND NOUNS

What if you have a compound noun, where more than one word is used to describe the noun? Look at these, for instance:

President of the student body
Brother-in-law

In cases like these, *always make the last word possessive*. So you would say:

The president of the student *body's* election campaign focused on improving cafeteria food.
Rosita loves her *brother-in-law's* car.

TWO FOR THE PRICE OF ONE

One last possession lesson: When you have more than one noun owning something, you also leave the possessive apostrophe for the last one mentioned:

Finally, I was psyched to have something to think about besides *Rosita and Charlie's* relationship.

CONTRACTIONS

Here's another time when the little apostrophe gets a big job. An apostrophe can actually replace letters to bring two words together into one:

does not becomes *doesn't*
I would becomes *I'd*
You will becomes *you'll*
. . . and more!

Just try not to use these contractions in your really formal pieces of writing, because it sounds more professional to use the full words.

CELEBRITY DEATH MATCH: IT'S VS. ITS

Ready for another warning about a common grammar mix-up? People *always* confuse these two words, and I can totally understand why. Just remember this:

- *It's* is a contraction of the words *it* and *is*: *It's* really dark outside.
- *Its* is a possessive pronoun: The cat has *its* own bed.

PLURALS

To make things even more fun (or, okay, maybe more confusing if you want to be all negative about it), apostrophes can be used to make certain kinds of nouns plural: numbers, letters, symbols, and words used as terms. It's perfectly acceptable to add -*s* by itself, but if you do choose to use -*'s*, put the noun you're pluralizing in italics, but leave the -*'s* in regular writing, like this:

What do all those #%@&'s in comics really stand for, anyway?
How many *cowabunga*'s do you think Bart Simpson has used?

In the second example, Bart Simpson isn't saying "cowabunga," and I'm not either. Instead, I'm pointing to the word *as a word*, which calls for italics, a little point of English usage you've been seeing all over the place in this book!

THE DASH

Ready to move on to another piece of punctuation? Great–time to talk about dashes! Dashes can substitute for colons, if you want to be a little flashy, and pairs of dashes can substitute for commas when you really want to emphasize a nonrestrictive element:

I'm always wishing I could be as confident–or at least as outgoing–as Rosita. Here's my chance!

TWO HYPHENS EQUAL ONE DASH

To make a dash, use two hyphens (--) without any space before or after them.

THE HYPHEN

Modifiers are the most needy parts of speech when it comes to hyphens. You'll need to put that short dash between words that are trying to act together as one adjective instead of independently:

Rosita is a well-known eye-catcher.

If you're uncertain about whether two modifiers should be compounded with a hyphen, try each word separately with the noun it's modifying. In Rosita's case, she's not a well eye-catcher *and* a known eye-catcher. The word *well* only makes sense when linked to *known*. (In fact, the word *well* is actually an adverb here, modifying the word *known*, not the noun *eye-catcher*.)

Don't use a hyphen if the adjective combo occurs after a linking verb such as *is*:

An eye-catcher, Rosita is well known.

Here, *well known* renames the subject and shouldn't be hyphenated.

Adverbs that announce themselves as adverbs—by ending in *-ly*, silly!—don't get hyphens either, since their part of speech is so easily spotted:

The easily spotted Rosita is an eye-catcher.

LET THE DICTIONARY CATCH YOUR EYE

Hyphens also go between the two ideas in some—but only some—compound nouns and verbs, like *cross-examine* and *twenty-five*. Which ones? I have three words for you: Look it up. I had to look up *eye-catcher*. You don't have to memorize which compound words get a hyphen, which get a space, and which just run all together. Let your dictionary store that information for you. Here are three hints, though: Fractions, numbers between 20 and 100, and words using the prefixes *all-*, *ex-*, and *self-* get hyphenated.

ELLIPSES

Here's a nice simple one for you: Ellipses are three equally spaced dots that show the reader that something is being left out. Usually, that something is from a quotation you're using, and it's important to use an ellipsis so that you're not just changing around what the speaker was saying:

In chapter 9 of Arianna's book about grammar, she writes, "Ellipses . . . show the reader that something is being left out."

PARTING IS SUCH SWEET SORROW. . . .

When you cut out the last part of a sentence you're quoting, you add a fourth dot to be the period. You can also use an ellipsis to show an unfinished thought. Of course, no one really recommends not finishing your thoughts, so limit yourself on this front and don't abuse ellipses, or else. . . .

PARENTHESES

Words you find in parentheses are sort of like second-class citizens in their sentences; the parentheses tell you that these words are less important. They sometimes just give you a definition of another part of your sentence, a different way to say it, or a little extra information. Check it out:

I'm a student at Paramus High School (PHS).

PUNCTUATION GOES OUTSIDE PARENTHESES

When the parenthetical part of your sentence comes at the end of the sentence, you put the period after the closing parenthesis, like I did right above. If it comes in the middle of the sentence and you need to use a comma after it's over, you put the comma after the closing parenthesis, too.

QUOTATION MARKS

We're down to quotation marks, your last piece of punctuation. Woo-hoo! The even better news is that the rules for quotation marks really aren't that hard. There are a few different times to use these.

DIRECT QUOTATIONS

When you're quoting someone directly, you use quotation marks on either side of the quoted words. You do this whether it's a full sentence or a few words, *as long as everything that's inside the quotation marks came directly from the speaker.* Here's an example:

"Are we done with the grammar lesson yet?" Rosita asked.
According to Rosita, grammar is "super-boring."

QUOTING PROSE OR POETRY

When you're quoting from a piece of prose or poetry in a paper you're writing, you use quotation marks as long as the quotation is fewer than four typed lines. If it's longer, then you set the quotation apart by starting it on its own line and indenting it ten spaces, and you don't use quotation marks. Here's an example of when to use quotation marks:

In Arianna's book about grammar, she writes, "When you're quoting from a piece of prose or poetry in a paper you're writing, you use quotation marks *as long as the quotation is fewer than four typed lines*."

When you're quoting poetry, the same four-line rule applies, but remember to put slashes between each of those lines so we can see where they are:

I've always loved these lines from one of the poems I read in my American Poetry class: "I cannot say what loves have come and gone, / I only know that summer sang in me / A little while, that in me sings no more."

TITLES

Here's a quick and easy one: Quotation marks go around titles of poems, short stories, articles, essays, and songs. Titles of longer works—books, magazines, albums—get italicized or underlined. Check it out:

> The lines I quoted above are from Edna St. Vincent Millay's poem "What Lips My Lips Have Kissed, and Where, and Why."
>
> "Oops! . . . I Did It Again" is the first song on Britney Spears's old album *Oops! . . . I Did It Again.*

QUOTATION PUNCTUATION

Sigh. Yes, it's true, you need to worry about the rest of the punctuation you're using inside and around quotation marks. But the rules here are pretty straightforward, too. Periods and commas that come at the end of quotes always go inside closing quotation marks, like this:

> "I can't believe you're still talking about quotation marks," Rosita said, "when we still have to figure out who your secret admirer is."

Question marks and exclamation points go inside the quotation marks if they're part of what the speaker said and outside if they're not. Check out these examples:

> Have you ever read Hemingway's short story "Hills Like White Elephants"?
>
> I got a lot of flak after writing a school newspaper article entitled, "Time to Reevaluate Sophomore English Curriculum?"

In the first example, my sentence as a whole is a question, but the title of Hemingway's short story isn't, so the question mark goes *outside* the closing quotation mark, away from the title. In the second sentence, the title of the article is a question but the sentence as a whole is not. The question mark goes *inside* the quotation marks *with* the title. Got it?

SINGLE QUOTATION MARKS

Single quotation marks are used when you have a quotation inside a quotation. Quotation. (It just felt like I hadn't used that word quite enough times there!) Check this out:

Before eventually agreeing to run my article, the school newspaper adviser warned me, “I’m not sure if we can use the title ‘Time to Reevaluate Sophomore English Curriculum?’ because it might upset the administration.”

YOUR TURN

Punctuate each of these sentences as needed.

1. Havent you read a short story called The Gift of the Magi

2. Its world famous author O Henry a pseudonym pen name for William Sydney Porter died when he was forty eight

3. The storys plot concerns a wife who sells her gorgeous hair in order to buy a watch chain for her husband

4. Meanwhile hes sold his highly valued watch to buy her you guessed it combs for her nonexistent hair

5. When we read it in English my quiz happy teacher wrote on the board Why is Henrys short story The Gift of the Magi so laden with irony

6. I wrote Each character has great motives but neither ends up with anything to show for it

7. The two characters gifts are useless and self defeating I continued

8. Then I wrote When you ask Why is Henrys short story laden with irony Ive got to point out how strong the couples love is for each other.

9. Theyre willing to give up their most valued possessions just because its Christmas

10. I concluded by asking Although you use the word irony isnt it romance not irony that keeps us reading The Gift of the Magi

* * * * *

As soon as we wrapped up our grammar lesson, Rosita opened her notebook to a clean sheet of paper and wrote the words *possible suspects* at the top of the page.

"Rosi, we're not talking about murderers here–just some guy who sent me an email."

"Do you want to solve the case or not?"

I realized it was going to be tough to stand in the way of Rosita's flair for the dramatic, so I let her make her list. Of course, it was pretty tough when we had basically zero clues–just a Gothic font and some goofy bat emoticons. Who was this guy?

"Maybe he's not worth all this, anyway," I said. "I mean, if he's, too shy to tell me who he is, then it's probably because there's something wrong with him."

"Are you serious? Arianna, can you say, 'hypocrite'? You're, like, the shyest girl I know when it comes to guys. At least he had the guts to send you this email. Look, why don't you start by writing back? You can send some messages back and forth to see if you like him or not."

"I guess you're right," I said.

After all, what could it hurt to write a couple of emails?

10

CHAPTER 10
GRAMMAR NO-NO'S

Over the next few days, my mysterious email friend was all I could think about. He'd replied almost immediately to my first email response, and soon we were trading messages back and forth all day long. The emails were getting longer and longer, too. I knew all about how he loved playing the saxophone but was worried his parents would make him give it up to concentrate on his schoolwork, and how his favorite book was *The Hitchhiker's Guide to the Galaxy* but his favorite writer was Stephen King.

He knew about my hobby of collecting Wonder Woman lunchboxes, and how I secretly liked listening to the oldies station when my parents were driving.

Most important, though, he knew my *name*. I still didn't know his! No matter how much I begged, he refused to tell me who he was. So finally I asked if we could meet in person before the dance. He agreed to meet me at the Sunset Diner in Paramus.

"What are you going to wear?" Rosita asked as soon as I told her.

I twirled the phone cord around my fingers, thinking about the contents of my closet. "I have no idea. Maybe you should come over and help me pick something out."

"No problem. Then you could help me with a card I'm making Charlie for his birthday. You know, just read it over to make sure I said everything right."

"Okay, I'll read it," I said. "But Rosi, I was thinking: From now on, you should really do this stuff yourself. I mean, you and Charlie are together now, and it's obvious he really likes you for you. Besides, I think you've learned a lot, you know?"

"I guess so. It's just that I'm still scared I'll mess something up. Didn't you say something about misunderstood magnifiers?"

I bit back a smile. "Misplaced modifiers," I said. "They're one of the easiest mistakes to make in grammar. Listen, why don't I give you one last lesson, and then, after that, you can write your own emails and letters to Charlie. Deal?"

"Deal."

We hung up, and I started rummaging through my dresser to pull out possible outfits for meeting my secret admirer. Somehow, grammar no-no's seemed like the perfect last topic for my lessons with Rosita, considering I was fresh from learning my *own* lesson of a different kind of no-no—falling for your friend's guy!

THE MODIFIER

We've seen a lot of modifiers so far, but just to review: **Modifiers** are words or phrases that—duh—*modify* another word in the sentence. Modifiers can be all different parts of speech, but what's important is that they give the words they're modifying more specific meaning, clarity, or detail. We've used the word *modifier* to describe adjectives, adverbs, prepositional phrases, clauses introduced by relative pronouns, and even whole clauses.

Sometimes it's hard to put modifiers in the right places in your sentences, so I'll give you some hints on how to make sure your modifiers are always just where they should be.

MODIFIER PLACEMENT

As you know, I'm pretty misplaced myself right now—I'm right in the middle of Charlie and Rosita's relationship, where everything is confusing! Modifiers can be misplaced, too, like in this example:

CONFUSING: *On Saturday* I wanted to choose the perfect outfit for my date.

In this sentence, it sounds like I'm going to choose my clothes on Saturday, when in fact Saturday is when I'll be wearing them! I put the prepositional phrase *on Saturday* too far away from the word it modifies, *date*. The goal with modifiers is to keep them close to the words they're modifying. If you don't, you could end up with a problem like this one. A little rearranging, and the sentence works much better:

BETTER: I wanted to choose the perfect outfit for my date *on Saturday*.

Sometimes a single word can trip you up:

CONFUSING: I *truly* wanted to choose the perfect outfit.

The word *truly* here is modifying the verb *wanted*, as if choosing an outfit were my sole purpose in life, but what I really mean to modify with the word *truly* is the perfect outfit:

BETTER: I wanted to choose the *truly* perfect outfit.

DANGLING MODIFIERS

Sometimes I feel like I have no purpose in life. But I guess I do—there's school to work hard in, my family to please, and Rosita to hang out with! Some modifiers, however, really don't have a purpose in life—or, at least, in the life of a sentence. (How sad!) They're desperately *trying* to modify something, but the thing they're trying to modify isn't there—or, at least, not where it's supposed to be. Check it out:

WRONG: *Trying on my favorite jeans,* they didn't meet my definition of perfection.

Why does the participial phrase *trying on my favorite jeans* have no purpose in the sentence? Well, it's modifying the pronoun *they*, but *they* refers back to the jeans. The jeans aren't trying themselves on—I'm trying *them* on! When a modifier hangs out at the beginning of a sentence but doesn't refer logically to anything *in* the sentence, it's called a **dangling modifier**. Let's get the pronoun *I* into the sentence so *trying on my favorite jeans* has something to modify:

RIGHT: *Trying on my favorite jeans, I* realized that they didn't meet my definition of perfection.

DISRUPTIVE MODIFIERS

These pushy modifiers keep sticking in where they don't belong in a sentence, interrupting the flow of things. (Sort of like I could do to Rosita and Charlie's relationship . . . if I wanted to be a troublemaker!) Like this:

WRONG: Jeans will *sometimes if they are left too long in the dryer,* shrink.
RIGHT: *Sometimes if they are left too long in the dryer,* jeans will shrink.

LIMITING AND SQUINTING MODIFIERS

It's always important to think about where you're putting your modifiers in a sentence, but it's extra crucial with these kinds of modifiers, because you can totally change the meaning of your sentence if you mess up.

LIMITING MODIFIERS

Sometimes, words need limits. Words have a tendency to spin out of control, getting crazier and crazier. . . . We need a certain kind of modifier to come to the rescue and set some boundaries. Words like *almost*, *even*, *just*, *merely*, and *only* are just the thing. They're called **limiting modifiers**, because they *limit* the meaning of the words they're modifying. These words should almost always go right before or right after the words being modified. Why? Because otherwise, you run into something like this:

WRONG: The Sunrise Diner *just* serves breakfast foods until noon.

Hmm, am I suggesting the diner serves the food but doesn't cook it or take it away? It seems so, because *just* wants to modify *serves*. Here are two possible fixes:

RIGHT: The Sunrise Diner serves *just* breakfast foods until noon.

Here I'm saying that you won't find lunch or dinner items, *just* breakfast foods.

RIGHT: The Sunrise Diner serves breakfast foods until *just* noon.

Here I'm saying that if you don't get to the diner by twelve, you can forget about those scrambled eggs!

SQUINTING MODIFIERS

These are modifiers that are so small, you have to squint to be able to see them. Ha–got you again! No, seriously, a **squinting modifier** is a modifier that could be modifying the word before or after it, which can obviously lead to more confusion. Here's an example:

WRONG: People who date *often* know what to wear.

The word *often* here could be modifying the verb *date* or the verb *know*. Depending on which it is, the sentence has two different meanings, so you have to determine the correct meaning and move the modifier accordingly:

RIGHT: People who *often* date know what to wear.

SPLIT INFINITIVES

The infinitive of a verb is the base form of the verb with the word *to* in front of it, like *to write, to eat,* or *to be.* Whenever you're using an infinitive in a sentence, you want to try not to split up the two parts by putting another word in between:

WRONG: I read an article in a magazine that said when you're on a date with a guy, you should be careful *to slowly eat* your food.

RIGHT: I read an article in a magazine that said when you're on a date with a guy, you should be careful *to eat* your food *slowly*.

Doesn't that second one sound much better?

PARALLEL CONSTRUCTION

Sometimes a sentence contains a series of modifiers strung together. The series could consist of adjectives, adjective clauses, subordinate clauses, or any other unit of grammar. In that situation, look at your sentence as if you're making a list. Everyone knows how to make a list, right? You line up all the words on your list and then toss a comma in after every word in the list except the last one:

Charlie and Rosita both love scary movies, disco, pistachio ice cream, and french fries.

Take another look at that example: All the words on that list are nouns. When you're making a list, do what you do when you're dressing up for a big date: Make sure everything on your list matches, from your shoes, to your skirt, to your sweater, to your ponytail holder. (Hey, on my list of things that match, every item is a prepositional phrase! Groovy, huh?) Look what happens when the items on your list *don't* match:

Charlie and Rosita both love scary movies, disco, pistachio ice cream, and to eat french fries.

That last item—*to eat french fries*—sticks out like a sore thumb. It's like wearing a striped shirt with plaid pants. Always double-check to be sure your sentence is perfectly coordinated.

LONG ITEMS IN A LIST

Sometimes the items in a list aren't so easy to identify, because the items themselves are pretty long:

> Off to the movies I went, after grabbing my books, rushing out of class, I piled into the car with my friends, and leaving my backpack right there on the sidewalk!

In this list, each item is a phrase, and in most cases the phrase begins with a present participle of a verb. But in one item, the phrase *does* have a subject: *I piled into the car with my friends*. It's a whole sentence, if you look at it by itself, unlike *rushing out of class* or *leaving my backpack right there on the sidewalk*. So let's take that subject right out and make it match the others:

> Off to the movies I went, after grabbing my books, rushing out of class, piling into the car with my friend, and leaving my backpack right there on the sidewalk!

There. That's better (except that my backpack is still sitting on the curb). Whenever you make a list, no matter how long each item on it or how short the list is itself, make sure each item uses the same kind of grammar as the other ones. It's called **parallelism**.

DOUBLE NEGATIVES

Get ready. . . . Here's one last lesson on a grammar no-no. Take a look at a line from a Rolling Stones song:

> I *can't* get *no* satisfaction.

Are the Stones trying to say that they're having trouble getting to a state of dissatisfaction? No way! They're trying to say that they want to be satisfied, but they're not. Sure, we know what they're *trying* to say. But two negatives together—like *can't* and *no* in that song—actually cancel each other out. People usually use two negatives to add emphasis, but what they're actually doing is changing the literal meaning of the sentence.

When two negatives appear together, you've got a **double negative**. To fix it, change one of the negatives to a positive:

I *can't* get *any* satisfaction.

Now we're talking!

YOUR TURN

Correct any misplaced, disruptive, dangling, or squinting modifiers and reunite any split infinitives in the following sentences.

1. After merely rejecting a hundred outfits, the one that looked best turned out to actually be a skirt, not jeans.

2. I am wearing it with a sweater and earrings over my leggings.

3. Rosita coached me, though my jeans were tempting, to definitely go with a skirt in a shade like an ocean on a rainy day of blue.

4. Trying to pick earrings, the right pair jumped almost out at me.

5. I decided my high-heeled boots, as key as footwear is, were the way to obviously go, and, when on my feet together with the skirt, Rosita agreed.

6. Boots mean leggings only to me.

7. The sweater to wear lastly Rosita found folding up all the rejected shirts.

8. A lighter shade of blue angora, on Saturday I'll wear it off the shoulder at the dance.

9. Though tolerable, after this ordeal I won't be spending time in my closet no longer.

Revise this sentence to make it parallel:

10. Although I'm glad to have assembled the perfect outfit, excited to wear it on Saturday, and it is thrilling to look good, I'm even happier to be out of my room at last.

* * * * *

Hopefully you're feeling as satisfied with your new grasp on grammar as Rosita was by the time we got through our final lesson. Are you wondering what happened to me on my blind date? Well, I guess I should fill you in, since you've been so patient.

I really wasn't sure what to expect when I walked into the Sunset Diner the next afternoon. I'd felt a connection with this guy in our emails, but what if it all fell apart in person? I didn't want to be too superficial, but looks matter. I knew you had to be attracted to someone to be happy going out with him.

"Arianna?"

I turned around in the direction of the voice, and my eyes bugged out in total shock. It was Theo! But wait—maybe he was there for some other reason and was just saying hi to be nice, since we'd hung out that one time with Charlie and Rosita.

"Um, hi," I said cautiously. "Are you . . . ?"

He smiled a shy, sweet smile, then pulled something out of the bag he was carrying and held it out to me.

You won't believe this one. Or maybe you will, if you're a sucker for these kinds of things. Theo had brought me a Wonder Woman lunchbox. Talk about a dream come true!

We sat down at a booth, ordered our food, and started talking. We were both a little nervous at first, but then we got comfortable and suddenly neither of us could shut up.

"So why didn't you tell me it was you?" I asked him. I didn't get it. Theo was adorable! There was no reason for a guy who looked like him to be embarrassed to admit his identity.

"Well, you didn't really seem that interested after we all went out," he said. "I could tell you were a cool girl, but you barely said anything to me. And besides, I guess I'm kind of shy on dates, so I know I didn't seem all that special. I thought we could get to know each other a little through email and then see what happened next."

Wow, he was dead on with that one. I hadn't given him a chance, and Rosita was right about my being a hypocrite. I'd written cute Theo off just because he was shy on the double date, when I'd been just as shy! Luckily, he'd given me another chance, a chance I wasn't about to pass up.

At precisely that moment, Charlie and Rosita walked into the diner and right up to our table.

"Um, sorry to barge in on your date, Arianna, but Charlie has a grammar problem he's trying to figure out, and when I told him you were an even bigger grammar whiz than I am, he insisted we come find you." Rosita seemed majorly embarrassed by the whole thing.

"It's so refreshing to meet a young woman with such terrific grammar," Charlie chirped.

I had trouble taking this all in. Charlie–the Charlie–wanted my help in grammar? This was too good to be true. Was I dreaming? But then I remembered–Rosita's my best friend forever. What did this guy think I was, some kind of grammar slut? Why were we all so worried about what he thought of our grammar, anyway?

"Hang on a minute, Charlie," I said. "Just why exactly are you so obsessed with good grammar?"

He looked embarrassed, his normally pallid cheeks flushing crimson. "Well, er—" he stammered. Finally, he blurted out: "It's because I'm really four hundred years old. I've had to endure a lot of bad grammar, and I like it when people get it right. I mean, how hard is it, really? But I get confused, because grammar rules keep changing. Why, when I was a lad—in Shakespeare's day, mind you—we could use the word "infer" where you would have to use "imply." But now that's a no-no. You see—"

"Charlie, shut the hell up! You're a bloodsucking ghoul. I can't believe I helped my BFF get together with you. Rosita, come on, we're leaving."

My grammar lessons with Rosita were officially over, but Theo had reminded me that, sometimes, what's true in grammar is true in life. Things aren't always what they seem, and there are exceptions to every rule!

CHAPTER 1

1. My friend / finally figured out the real purpose of grammar.
2. Good grammar skills and football games / help you to meet guys.
3. Rosita, who was never a huge grammar fan, / was afraid to write Charlie an email.
4. Sentence fragment:~~Because~~ Rich / warned Rosita about using good grammar. ORBecause Rich warned Rosita about using good grammar, she / was too nervous to write Charlie.
5. Being a good friend, I / agreed to give a little crash course in clauses to Rosita.
6. A friendship that also helps your grammar) / is pretty rare.
7. Giving advice / works both ways, though, with Rosita and me.
8. On the subject of clothes, Rosita / has opinions to spare and shares them freely.
9. Her long hair flipped over her shoulder, Rosita / rummages through my closet, talking about my sweaters but actually looking for something cool to borrow.
10. Rosita / is talented at meeting guys and seldom sits home on a Saturday night, but she / is never, ever, the slightest bit stuck on herself.

CHAPTER 2

1. She doesn't like to admit it to most people [common, concrete], but Rosita [proper, concrete]has a huge collection [common, concrete]of stuffed animals [concrete, common]from Toys "R" Us [proper, concrete].
2. I have lived in the town [concrete, common]of Paramus [proper, cmmon] for my whole life [common, abstract].
3. My favorite television [common, concrete]show [common, concrete], Joan of Arcadia [proper, concrete], airs on Friday [proper, abstract]nights [common, concrete].
4. My sister [common, concrete], Marie [proper, concrete], worships Social Studies [proper, abstract]and wants to be a CNN [proper, concrete] reporter [common, concrete], traveling to exotic countries [common, concrete]like Ethiopia [proper, concrete]and Pakistan [proper, concrete].

5. phones
6. knives
7. kisses
8. armies
9. alumni

CHAPTER 3

1. My friends Sonya and Kaitlin like to ask for my help with their English homework.
2. Between you and me, they don't really need help, but whom would I spend fourth period with, if not them?
3. Today, Sonya said, "Kat and I will never catch up with your English crowd, even though it moves pretty slowly!"
4. I shot back, "Every science nerd I know has to tell his or her little English nerd joke, even though jokes about science nerds are far more common than ones about us English types!"
5. Neither Sonya nor her science-nerd friends have made their English nerd jokes funny enough for anyone else to remember, much less laugh, so I can't tell you any of them.
6. Everyone in fourth period has ~~their~~ his or her own opinion about Sonya's jokes, which strike only ~~she~~ her as hilarious.
7. It seems obvious that ~~me~~ she and ~~her~~ I have wildly different ideas of funny, but when a Chemistry quiz is staring ~~ourselves~~ us in the face, nobody is laughing ~~their~~ his or her head off, not even Sonya.
8. Chemistry and English both have ~~its~~ their good points, being interesting to ~~I~~ me, challenging, and good preparation for college, but, as you probably guessed, the easiest courses are not ~~them~~ they.
9. I guess I'd rather spend fourth period listening to Sonya's terrible jokes, each of us studying for whatever we have next, than spend it with a truly hilarious person who has ~~their~~ his or her own friends and ~~who~~ whom we aren't truly friends with, either.
10. Much—maybe all—of her goofiness is actually lovable, when you consider Sonya as ~~their~~ its good-hearted source, and though her taste in jokes may be dismal, her taste in friendship is fabulous.

CHAPTER 4

1. Rosita and my friendship *has persevered* through thick and thin.
2. Until I *met* her, I *had had* no genuine best friend.
3. I *thought* I *knew* what *made* a friendship, but I *was kidding* myself.
4. One of my friends from middle school, Lena, *cheered* me up after I *had bombed* a quiz, for example, and I *did* the same when her gerbil *was dying*, but I never *spent* the kind of time with Lena that Rosita and I *spend* together.
5. By next June, I *will have been* friends with Rosita for three years.
6. We *are going* strong.
7. Since you *have followed* my story so avidly, you *know* how great Rosita *is*.
8. Now I *am using* the word *friend* more carefully.
9. Don't *forget* to pass on any great boyfriend-getting ideas you *happen* to have.
10. I *will need* them, as you *will have seen* by the time you finish this book!

CHAPTER 5

1. Every appetizer and entrée at T.G.I. Friday's costs about the same.
2. Unlike some other restaurants I enjoy, here neither the onion rings nor the tostada is overpriced.
3. The staff definitely hate their jobs, though.
4. Rosita and Charlie, as well as Theo and me, try to be as nice as possible because the company of waiters keeps shrinking and we don't have our nachos yet.
5. After all those potato skins and nachos comes an ice-cream brownie, Death by Chocolate.
6. *Will and Grace* plays on the TV behind the booth, and the Dixie Chicks blare on the jukebox.
7. Country, bluegrass, or swing music gets my vote for most boring, and this date gets my vote for most awkward.
8. Are *awkward* and *boring* the right words for what I feel?
9. Although we risked more surly service, Rosita and I ordered desserts.

10. Theo said nothing to suggest that he would enjoy a taste of my Death by Chocolate.

CHAPTER 6

1. Rosita, who is brilliant [describing] at post-date [describing] analysis, knows that I like thick, [describing] curly [describing], dark [describing] hair, but Theo is only one [quantifying] among many [quantifying] guys with a [article] head of terrific [describing] hair.
2. Charlie has that [identifying] kind of hair, too.
3. When several [quantifying] guys have fabulous [describing] hair, I am going to go for the [article] one who is smartest [describing/superlative], funniest [describing/superlative], and most interesting [describing/superlative] under his [possessive pronoun] hair.
4. Which of those [identifying] two [quantifying] guys fits that [identifying] bill better [*better* is a comparative adverb–not an adjective]
5. I have got to stop thinking so [adverb, modifies *often*] often [adverb, modifies *thinking*] about Charlie, his [adjective, modifies *hair*] great [adjective, modifies *hair*] hair, and his [adjective, modifies *personality*] smart [adjective, modifies *personality*], funny [adjective, modifies *personality*], interesting [adjective, modifies *personality*] personality.
6. Obsession is not [adverb, modifies *good*] good [adjective, modifies *obsession*], and I've got it badly [change bad, an adjective, *badly*, an adverb, which modifies *got*].
7. An [adjective, modifies *bystander*] innocent [adjective, modifies *bystander*] bystander might even [adverb, modifies *might say*] say my [adjective, modifies *case*] case of [misplaced adjective, modifies *obsession*] obsession is extreme [adjective, modifies *case*], and Rosita's [adjective, modifies *obliviousness*] obliviousness makes it ~~more~~ worse [adverb, modifies *makes*].
8. Shake your [adjective, modifies *head*] head sadly [adverb, modifies *shake*], and get your [adjective, modifies *sympathy*] ~~most~~ deepest [adjetive, modifies *sympathy*] sympathy out [adverb, modifies *get*], too [adverb, modifies *get your deepest sympathy out*], because my [adjective,

modifies *obsession*] obsession is going nowhere fast [adverb, modifies *is going*].

9. Crushes are worse than bad hair days, but, let's face it, less horrible than cancer.
10. When it comes to my worst nightmare, losing Rosita's friendship, the simplest solution of all would be to forget Charlie as soon as possible.

CHAPTER 7

1. I hope Rosita will stop asking for my help (modifies *asking*) on her emails (modifies *help*) after this date (modifies *stop*), for I am getting tired of writing them (modifies *tired, writing them* is a noun phrase).
2. On the other hand (modifies *can't wait*), I can't wait for my Toasters CD (modifies *wait*) from her (modifies *Toasters CD*).
3. Through their catchy tunes (modifies *musicians*), that group of musicians (modifies *group*) makes me feel like dancing and singing (modifies *feel*).
4. After all that ice cream (modifies *will need*), I'll need to dance all night, just to return to my normal size (modifies *return*).
5. To Ben & Jerry's (modifies *Marie and I*), Marie and I have got to be the ideal customer, with our dedication (modifies *Marie and I*) to finishing whole cartons (modifies *dedication, finishing whole cartons* is a noun phrase) of the stuff (modifies *cartons*).
6. Marie thought [that (SC) we should stop after (PP) the mac-and (CC)-cheese], but (CC) I decided [that (SC) we needed to finish with (PP) something healthy], [since (SC) we were feeling guilty].
7. Either (CR) Marie or (CR) I should have made the fridge off (PP) limits after (PP) the mac-and (CC)-cheese.
8. Instead (DP), we kept eating those kinds of (PP) food [until (SC) midnight came and (CC) went].
9. After (PP) midnight, Marie and (CC) I pigged out (PP) in (RP) our pj's, which (SC) were more comfortable [than our jeans had been].
10. Marie, [whom (SC) I usually admire for (PP) her healthy eating habits], taught me a thing or (CC) two about (PP) junk food and (CC) being bummed.

CHAPTER 8

1. Who knew that I would become the voice of Rosita?
2. Not only am I writing her emails, but, yikes, I'm actually asking Charlie to get serious with her!
3. That kind of forwardness, which I don't normally have, would be really handy in certain situations: telling off Sara; explaining myself to my mother when I'm late; and, of course, going after Charlie way back in seventh grade.
4. When I think of all the time I've wasted being shy, I blame me, not anyone else, because there's no one else to blame, is there?
5. I'll have to kiss all those opportunities I had goodbye: the sweetheart dance on April 15, 1999; the sock hop in November 2000; and the Fourth of July party at 35 Dayton Way, Paramus, New Jersey.
6. What I should do now, if I can relocate my sanity, is take a nice long deep breath and say, "Arianna, you've come a long way, baby!"
7. "You might be a little shy, but you've got a great friend in Rosita," I'll continue, feeling better.
8. Next, I suppose I'll eat all the ice cream that I can find, and, finally, my heartache will be gone.
9. I'll let you know if any of this stuff works after I do it, okay?
10. Don't hold your breath, though; it seems like a long shot.

CHAPTER 9

1. Haven't you read a short story called "The Gift of the Magi"?
2. Its world-famous author, O. Henry, [*or dash*] a pseudonym (pen name) for William Sydney Porter, [*or dash*] died when he was forty-eight.
3. The story's plot concerns a wife who sells her gorgeous hair in order to buy a watch chain for her husband.
4. Meanwhile, he's sold his highly valued watch to buy her—you guessed it—combs for her nonexistent hair.
5. When we read it in English, my quiz-happy teacher wrote on the board, "Why is Henry's short story 'The Gift of the Magi' so laden with irony?"

6. I wrote, "Each character has great motives but neither ends up with anything to show for it."
7. "The two characters' gifts are useless and self-defeating," I continued.
8. Then I wrote, "When you ask, 'Why is Henry's short story laden with irony?' I've got to point out how strong the couple's love is for each other."
9. They're willing to give up their most valued possessions just because it's Christmas.
10. I concluded by asking, "Although you use the word *irony,* isn't it romance, not irony, that keeps us reading 'The Gift of the Magi?'"

CHAPTER 10

1. After ~~merely~~ rejecting *merely* a hundred outfits, the one that looked best *actually* turned out to ~~actually~~ be a skirt, not jeans.
2. I am wearing it *over my leggings,* with a sweater and earrings ~~over my leggings~~.
3. *Though I was tempted to wear my jeans,* Rosita coached me ~~though my jeans were tempting,~~ *definitely* to ~~definitely~~ go with a skirt in a shade *of blue* like an ocean on a rainy day ~~of blue~~.
4. *As I was* trying to pick earrings, the right pair *almost* jumped ~~almost~~ out at me.
5. *As key as footwear is,* I decided my high-heeled boots ~~as key as footwear is,~~ were *obviously* the way to ~~obviously~~ go, and, when *she saw them* on my feet together with the skirt, Rosita agreed.
6. Boots mean *only* leggings ~~only~~ to me.
7. *Lastly,* the sweater to wear ~~lastly~~ Rosita found *while she was* folding up all the rejected shirts.
8. ~~A lighter shade of blue angora,~~ *At the dance* on Saturday, I'll wear ~~it~~ *the sweater, which is a lighter shade of blue angora,* off the shoulder ~~at the dance~~.
9. Though *it was* tolerable, after this ordeal I won't be spending time in my closet ~~no~~ *any* longer. OR Though tolerable, ~~after~~ this ordeal *means that* I won't be spending time in my closet ~~no~~ *any* longer.

10. Although I'm glad to have assembled the perfect outfit, excited to wear it on Saturday, and ~~it is thrilling~~ *thrilled* to look good, I'm even happier to be out of my room at last.